THE
WORK

A Paperback Original
First published 1989 by
Poolbeg Press Ltd.
Knocksedan House,
Swords, Co. Dublin, Ireland.

ISBN I 85371-037-7

Cover design by Pomphrey Associates

Printed by The Guernsey Press Ltd.,
Vale, Guernsey, Channel Islands.

THE
WORK

An Investigation into the History of Opus Dei and how it operates in Ireland Today

Fergal Bowers

POOLBEG

Fergal Bowers was born in Dublin in 1961. Since 1980 he has worked in Ireland as a journalist and has produced reports for the *Irish Times*, the *Evening Press* and the *Evening Herald*. He has participated in RTE's *Morning Ireland* and the Pat Kenny *Today at Five* radio programmes in connection with exclusive news stories. He specialises in investigative journalism and now works as a senior journalist with an Irish newspaper.

For Roz,
who has given me years
of love and support

Author's Note

From the outset it must be stated that the author is not suggesting or implying that any of the persons named in this book are members of Opus Dei, at whatever level, unless this is specifically stated. Nor is the author suggesting or implying that any of the persons or companies named in this book know or approve of the activities or methods of recruitment of Opus Dei.

The author and publishers would like to thank those who gave permission to quote from their copyright material. If any involuntary infringement of copyright has occurred, sincere apologies are offered and the owner of such copyright is requested to contact the publishers.

Those wishing to enter into correspondence with the author on matters raised in this book, or those with additional information on Opus Dei, may contact the author by writing to the publishers.

*This book is dedicated to the memory of
my late father, to my mother, brothers,
family and all my friends.*

Foreword

This book came into being as a result of conversations I had with anxious parents and individuals concerning the work and practices of Opus Dei in Ireland. Little is known of Opus Dei (translated from Latin as the work of God) by the general public. Often what is known is surmise and conjecture, based on snippets of information, media controversy and sensationalism. As a journalist my aim in this book is to explore the facts and present a truthful and balanced portrait of this relatively new movement.

Opus Dei is possibly the most influential lay organisation within the Roman Catholic Church today. World-wide it claims over 80,000 members of eighty different nationalities. The organisation has major influence in the Vatican and its headquarters are in Rome. Opus Dei enjoys the active support of Pope John Paul II, who declared the organisation the Church's first ever "Personal Prelature" in 1982—a legal framework made possible by Vatican II. In essence this gave Opus Dei a very special status within the church.

For Opus Dei the new status justified its claim to originality and made the organisation a recognised part of the constitution of the Roman Catholic Church. Opus Dei is so far the only entity in the Catholic Church to be accorded this status. With the "Personal Prelature," Opus

Dei was given its own bishop, the "President General" who has world-wide jurisdiction over the spiritual work and organisation of its members.

This move made it independent of the Irish clergy or any other national clergy and answerable directly to Rome and to the Pope. Moves are underway by supporters of Opus Dei inside and outside the Vatican to have the movement's Spanish founder, Monsignor Josemaría Escrivá de Balaguer, beatified and canonised.

Opus Dei likes to think of itself as a family or, in another way, as a "disorganised organisation" with a definite structure but a minimum of red tape and bureaucracy. The basic message of *The Work* , as members refer to it, is the universal call to holiness emphasised by Vatican II. One of the basic teachings of Vatican II was that everyone is called to do God's work in their daily lives, implementing Christian values and the teachings of Christ in everything they do.

Opus Dei's work involves making Catholics (and non-Catholics) more aware of the importance of sanctity in daily living and of serving God in ordinary work. It also believes in vigorously adhering to and promoting traditional Roman Catholic teaching. How this is achieved will be the subject of this book.

Ireland, with over 1,000 Opus Dei members, is of particular interest and importance to the organisation in a world-wide context. It provides the movement at ground level with a large pool of well-educated, English speaking Roman Catholics—some of whom after joining *The Work* will move on to other countries to promote the organisation's cause. Ireland has always been regarded as one of the last bastions of traditional and authentic Roman Catholic teaching.

I hope this book will give the public a wider

knowledge of what Opus Dei is about. Finally, I would like to thank all those who put up with a barrage of questions, and others who provided me with confidential personal information and documents. In as few as necessary cases, names have been changed to protect sources or respect privacy, but only after I have been satisfied as to the validity of the information.

Dublin, 1989

Contents

Without the freedom to criticise,
no praise has any value

Chapter 1

In the Name of God

Opus Dei is primarily a lay Catholic organisation, founded in Spain in 1928. Its members dedicate themselves to a life of commitment and strict spiritual discipline in serving God in their daily work. The basic principle is simple: anyone can achieve holiness by offering their daily work to God. Membership demands an extra commitment and involves a belief that only traditional Roman Catholic teaching will save the world from damnation. Opus Dei members take their mission very seriously and most turn over some or all of their income to the organisation. While the high-ranking members practise celibacy as part of their commitment, many other members choose voluntarily to abide by the bond of poverty and chastity. A large number of Opus Dei members are married and contribute some of their income to the movement.

The organisation is headed up by a President General (the prelate) at present Monsignor Alvaro del Portillo, a Spanish priest who worked with Opus Dei's founder Monsignor Josemaría Escrivá before his death in 1975. Opus Dei also has about 1,200 clerical members who act as chaplains and advisers to the world-wide membership, claimed to be over 80,000. All matters concerning the internal administration of Opus Dei, the spiritual commitments of its members, and the selection of its priests come under the direct authority of Monsignor Alvaro del Portillo. His powers are similar to those of a Superior General of a religious order although it must be stressed that Opus Dei is not a religious order. Only 2 per cent of its members are priests. While its members are answerable to the President General as regards their specific commitments to Opus Dei, they remain under the jurisdiction of their local diocesan bishop in all matters which the church lays down regarding the broad mass of the Catholic faithful. However, no matter how strongly Opus Dei seeks to deny the fact, its recently acquired status as a "Personal Prelature" means that it sometimes slips out of the control of local Irish bishops and priests.

The main work of the movement is to spread the life-plan of holiness in daily living among people of all walks of life, but especially among those with high educational standards. Members of every profession belong to Opus Dei: doctors, lawyers, university professors, journalists, publishers, bankers, engineers, politicians—people of all ages from across the social spectrum. Individuals join Opus Dei after a training period of about six months, having become familiar with the spiritual teachings of the founder. The formal process of joining is by a written contract whereby the person joining promises to abide by the spiritual teachings of the organisation.

The movement today has over 700 journalists as members, including the head of the Vatican Press Office, Joaquin Navarro-Vallis. It also has 487 university lecturers and schoolteachers amongst its ranks. When people hear of "vocations" to Opus Dei they expect to see some kind of religious order or at least some external signs in the members to identify their association with Opus Dei. However, the truth is that Opus Dei members do not particularly advertise their membership but view it as a matter of private conscience. They do not wear badges, ties or special clothing that publicly declare their allegiance to God's work. Opus Dei members will not be found singing and dancing, preaching their faith on city streets or knocking on doors in the suburbs (as some sects do) in order to recruit people. Membership is clearly seen as something private and personal and not for public scrutiny.

As an institution, Opus Dei exists to provide its members with spiritual guidance and support for their life of piety, together with the theological and apostolic teaching given by Opus Dei priests. The life-plan includes daily Mass, regular Confession and Holy Communion, spiritual reading, prayers, reciting the Rosary and seeking potential recruits for the movement. As lay people in a wide variety of jobs, members of Opus Dei can penetrate society in ways that the clergy can *not*.

The image Opus Dei presents to the world is of an organisation whose main work is carried out by each member personally in his or her daily effort to make the teaching of Christ known by word and deed. The organisation insists that its aims are purely spiritual and that they do not concern themselves with individual members' private occupations or personal lives. Opus Dei says that members enjoy the same freedom as other Catholic citizens in their professional work, social, political and financial activities and that the Opus Dei-run university residence centres, youth clubs, conference centres, retreats and seminars are only for the purposes of promoting the spirit of the work.

In reality, Opus Dei acts as a small but very powerful pressure group, publicly declaring its members' independence but in reality assured of mobilising their support against the evils they have identified as a threat to public morals and the institutions of the Church—evils like divorce, contraception, abortion, secular humanism, pluralism and liberal tendencies in society, especially socialism and communism. The movement is ultra-conservative and some of its members have been directly involved in other organisations such as the Pro-Life Amendment Campaign in Ireland, SPUC (the Society for the Protection of the Unborn child), the Anti-Divorce Campaign and Family Solidarity. All of these are right-wing conservative pressure groups which have played a key role in Irish society especially during recent referenda.

Undoubtedly the vast majority of those who join Opus Dei are impelled by a strong religious conviction and a belief in the necessity of protecting society from the aforementioned "evils." But Opus Dei's activities have been a cause of anxiety to many Catholics (and non-Catholics) who disagree with its approach to Catholicism. The covert nature of the organisation and its unwillingness to give any real information are self-defeating. For example, the constitutions of Opus Dei are not available to the general public but solely to the elite and "high" ranking members within the movement. Opus Dei have said that since the organisation has received the blessing of Pope John Paul II the constitutions have been given to the bishops of all the diocese where Opus Dei operate. This author is aware of a number of Irish bishops who have never seen the constitutions and who have grave reservations about the work of Opus Dei. The internal Opus Dei magazine *Cronica* is not available outside of the organisation. The internal structure remains secret and the business ventures which the movement or its members control are not revealed. The names of Opus Dei members who are directors on the boards of banks, insurance companies, international corporations, or work in the civil service or political life are confidential. In the constitution of Opus Dei, Article 191 states: "The numeraries and supernumeraries must be convinced of the need to maintain a prudent silence regarding the names of other members and never reveal to anyone the fact that they belong to Opus Dei." In addition Article 189 includes the statement "... in order to achieve its aims more easily, the Institute must live in concealment." Is it any surprise then that the movement leaves itself open to accusations of intense secrecy and freemasonry?

Two separate branches exist within Opus Dei—one for men and the other for women. The two sexes are rigidly segregated with separate Opus Dei residence centres for men and women. The priests come from among the lay membership of the organisation, reach the priesthood after completing their ecclesiastical studies and are called to Holy Orders by the President General of Opus Dei. The Priestly Society of the Holy Cross is the body within Opus Dei which is open to priests ordained in any diocese who wish to exercise their ministry in accordance with the teachings of the movement. Their membership is not supposed to affect their accountability to their own diocesan bishop who in theory continues to be their superior. But such a situation must inevitably result in divided loyalties on occasions.

Membership of Opus Dei is broken up into four categories, essentially different levels of commitment: these are numeraries, associates, supernumeraries and co-operators.

The highest rank in general membership is that of a numerary. These people are the full-time members of the organisation, often described within the movement as those with a "higher vocation." They donate their full salaries to Opus Dei and in return the organisation provides them with a living allowance. Outside of their professional work, numeraries dedicate all of their time to the promotion and administration of Opus Dei. Many go on to become "spiritual directors" in the various residence centres around Ireland. This involves counselling individual members at regular get-togethers. The most obvious difference between numeraries and supernumeraries is that the former are required to live in Opus Dei residences on a permanent basis. Numeraries can be male or female. Constitution article number 53 of Opus Dei states that "for the numeraries, incorporation into the institute demands the pronunciation of the vows proper to the society of poverty, chastity and obedience." Opus Dei insists that vows are no longer taken but that intending members pledge themselves to the "spirit of Opus Dei." The organisation wishes to differentiate the movement from and avoid any comparison with religious orders whose members take specific vows.

In order to join Opus Dei, the intending member signs a contract binding him to the rules and obligations as laid down by the President General. In return the organisation undertakes to provide the number with spiritual guidance, religious formation and pastoral attention by the clergy of Opus Dei. In general the numeraries have a high standard of education and constitute about ten per cent of the total membership. The first move towards membership is to write to the "father" (the founder) in Rome requesting admission. After a six-month trial period a provisional commitment is given and renewed each year until the organisation is satisfied that the intending member has shown a full understanding of the essence and responsibilities of Opus Dei and is ready for a permanent contract of membership. A person can only sign such a contract if he or she is over eighteen and then only for a year at a time. Full life membership is only possible at the age of twenty-three. However, it must be stressed that many people come into contact and are deeply involved in the movement from an early age through junior youth clubs run by Opus Dei members. There is no younger age limit set before which recruitment cannot begin. Full members are free to request termination of the contract by writing to the President General. This will usually be given but not before every human effort is made to persuade the person to stay. Legally there are no financial penalties for people who terminate their contract.

All those who live within the residence centres are bound in absolute obedience to their spiritual director, the head of the centre. According to the Opus Dei internal magazine, "blind obedience to your superiors is the way to sanctification" (*Cronica* VIII, 1963); "eat, sleep and forget that you exist" (*Cronica* VII, 1966) and "our ego has died and our only concern is the collective ideal of uniting our efforts towards the same end" (*Cronica* XI, 1954).

The spiritual director ensures that all numeraries follow a strict programme of self-mortification. This involves self-flagellation or whipping the buttocks with a roped whip called the *discipline*. Members usually do this once a week. Another form of self-punishment involves the wearing of a spiked chain called the *cilis* which is worn on the upper thigh for about two hours each day, except on holy days.

Self-mortification is a recognised part of personal penance and has been practised down through the centuries. Opus Dei insists that it has to be viewed in the whole context of religious devotion. Members who use these unusual devices swear by the purifying virtues of the *cilis* and the *discipline*. Opus Dei says that such practices are not engaged in until a member has reached a sufficiently developed state of spiritual awareness and understands the full meaning of the exercises. One would have thought that men and women in our modern world are suffering sufficient pain for it to be unnecessary for them to chastise further their inner and outer selves in such a physically painful manner. But as one young Opus Dei member pointed out, whipping oneself is infinitely more worthwhile and a lot less painful than jogging for ten miles or taking part in some strenuous sporting activity.

The numeraries lead a life of devotion and prayer. They are separated from their families and take few holidays outside the centres of Opus Dei work. Most aspects of their lives are rigidly controlled and in the residence centres little privacy can be expected. Former numeraries have claimed that correspondence is vetted and reading material carefully censored. Television viewing is usually restricted to the news, likewise radio. Any contact with the outside world—including contact with parents and friends—must be approved. Most books, films and newspapers are censored.

The associates take the same vows as the numeraries but they do not always live in the residence centres. They usually come from relatively modest social backgrounds and fulfil a largely menial role in the organisation. Most associates are women and are sometimes referred to as the "little sisters of the professional numeraries." Many come from Opus Dei-run catering colleges to work in the residence centres. The women associates clean and cook in both the male and female Opus Dei residences. Because the men do not involve themselves in domestic work, the women are brought in early in the morning while male members are still in their rooms. Many of the younger girls who become associates remain as such no matter what their age or experience. For these associates there is little possibility of developing a talent or furthering their education except insofar as it will serve Opus Dei.

Such male/female discrimination was a characteristic of Spanish society in the 1920s when the movement was founded and even in Spain today Opus Dei's numerary ladies wear white, have their own chapel and sleep on boards. The female associates cook, clean and wear blue. They sleep on ordinary beds because, curiously, Opus Dei believes that the "ladies" will have sexual fantasies if they sleep on soft beds while the associates will sink to sleep, exhausted and untempted after a hard day's work.

A young girl from Donegal who stayed at the Opus Dei Glenard University Residence Centre in Dartry, Dublin, explained the atmosphere in the centre in a letter to the author.

> My sister and I entered Glenard at fifteen and left at the age of seventeen. We worked in the catering department at Glenard for the two years from 7.30 am to 7.30 pm, seven days a week. If we were lucky we had two weeks holidays each year. However, in Glenard we were not allowed to watch television except to see the news. Books, magazines and radio were forbidden and we were not allowed out to the gate on our own except when a member of Opus Dei accompanied us. Telephone calls were forbidden and some of our incoming calls were listened in on. In the first year Mass was compulsory each day. When we were seventeen we travelled with some Opus Dei members to Rome so as they might convince us to join during the holiday. They paid for our visit.

The supernumerary members comprise a large proportion of the total Opus Dei membership worldwide. Supernumeraries do not live in the houses of residence and many are married. They are the real power-base of the movement, often working in very influential positions in society where they have the opportunity to bring in a large number of recruits. Supernumeraries pledge obedience to Opus Dei and donate a sizeable amount of their income to the movement.

The lowest level on the scale of membership are the co-operators. They take no formal vows. Their role is in assisting Opus Dei in its activities and growth. Fund-raising plays a major part in this. One priest I spoke to thought Opus Dei was "some kind of charity" after he discovered that they were running a cake sale and a bazaar in his parish. Co-operators can be of any religious persuasion because the basic premise is that their religious beliefs come secondary to their ability to raise money.

Through their positions of influence and individual contributions, the co-operators provide operational cash flow for Opus Dei. The only people excluded from membership of Opus Dei at co-operator level are communists and freemasons.

There are no elections within Opus Dei except for the office of President General. All other positions are by his appointment. The founder, Monsignor Escrivá, claimed infallibility in all matters of Opus Dei, according to ex-spiritual director Dr John Roche, and as a condition of membership all are obliged to believe in his divine inspiration. The weekly meeting with the spiritual director, which all members are required to attend, is the movement's greatest means of control. It is organised and specifically intended to stamp obedience into all members. Each Opus Dei residence centre has a spiritual director who is the head numerary.

According to Dr Denys Turner, a former Opus Dei Director in Dublin and now a lecturer in theology at Bristol University,

> you go and talk to the spiritual director and are put under very great pressure to say absolutely everything that could possibly be relevant to your own progress as a Christian. You have to accept what he or she says by way of advice as literally being the word of God. Much discussion would frequently involve matters of very great intimacy, things which go very deep into your own personality. In this way Opus Dei exercises a hold over a person at the deepest level through these weekly personal meetings.

Opus Dei members do not go to ordinary priests for Confession. Instead they visit an Opus Dei priest, of whom there are fifteen in Ireland, one living in each of the residence centres around the country. The idea of using an Opus Dei priest is geared towards the internal cohesion of the organisation because it is believed that an ordinary priest might not fully understand the nature and the role of the Opus Dei movement. According to the internal magazine, *Cronica* (VI, 1962) under *La Confesion* :

> You will go to your brothers (the Opus Dei priests) as I go for Confession. If we were to go to a person who could only cure our wound superficially ... it would be because we are cowards ... and in doing so is wrong, seeking a second-hand doctor who cannot give us more than a few seconds of his time ... it would also harm the work. You would not sin

because of this, but woe to you ... you would have
begun to hear of the bad shepherd.

This bears up ex-members' claims of the Opus Dei
distrust of "ordinary priests." Furthermore, the
organisation teaches, "the evil comes from within and
from very high up ... There is an authentic rottenness, and
at times it seems as if the mystical body of Christ were a
corpse in decomposition that stinks." (*Cronica* II, (1972).
A book published in Barcelona by Maria Moreno entitled
El Opus Dei says the following: "But within the
organisation...the directors possess because of being
united with the Father (Opus Dei's founder) the gift of
infallibility" and on page 61 of the same book, "we are
those of the people who remain faithful to God, and the
only ones who save the church in this age."

Opus Dei does itself a disservice in its dangerous claims
to near-exclusive truth and group superiority. These
beliefs tend to alienate it from other God-fearing Roman
Catholics including the clergy. However, while in private
some Irish priests and bishops have expressed their
concern over certain aspects of Opus Dei's activities, most
are loath to speak out publicly as any public criticism
would appear to be indirectly criticising the judgement of
Pope John Paul II who has given the movement his
blessing.

Perhaps the most common feature of religious groups is
their missionary zeal and persuasive recruitment
methods. Opus Dei expends huge efforts in the business
of spreading its special message and the principles of the
founder, and making what it views as disciples. Listen to
the words of Monsignor Escrivá, the Spanish founder.
"We do not have any other aim than the corporate one;
proselytism, winning vocations," from *Cronica* V, 1963.

Other remarks are also valuable in giving an insight into the movement's aims. "Go out into the highways and byways and push those whom you find to come and fill my house, force them to come in, push them…you must kill yourself for proselytism" (*Cronica* IV, 1971). Ex-members have described how recruitment methods are taught and practised as a high art; how "holy coercion" is used and some parents and friends of members are kept unaware of what is going on until their son or daughter has already taken the decision to join.

Fr Andrew Byrne, an Opus Dei priest, told the *Daily Mail* on 14 January 1981, "In some cases when a youngster says he wants to join, we do advise them not to tell their parents. This is because the parents do not understand us."

In a reply to media criticism about the specific issue of whether there may be a conflict between parents and Opus Dei, Paul Harman, the official spokesman for Opus Dei in Ireland said:

> My personal experience suggests that many such problems can be resolved through a deeper reflection on the honour of having a son or daughter follow an authentic vocation in the service of Christ and the Church.
>
> (*Irish Independent*, Letters to the Editor,
> 22 December 1986)

Opus Dei is not always to blame where there is conflict between parents and the organisation. Intending members often fail to involve their parents in their decision to join until it is a *fait accompli*. The sudden, unannounced change of loyalties to the "new family of Opus Dei" can have an utterly devastating effect on naturally concerned and later bewildered parents. Much more openness is needed on both sides to solve this cruel problem. Other difficulties arise in regard to commitments to the movement. The vow of poverty often means not being able to give presents on birthdays or at Christmas. Numerary members, especially, often have difficulty in getting permission to attend family weddings or get-togethers as a result of the heavy restrictions on their social lives.

What happens to those who decide to leave Opus Dei? The movement says that the door is always open for those who wish to leave and have themselves released from the bond which is basically a spiritual one (though the contract is in writing). However, ex-members claim to have suffered severe withdrawal symptoms, fear and guilt on leaving the movement. The words of the founder are not very consoling :

> If one of my children abandons the fight, or leaves the war, or turns his back, let him know that he betrays us all, Jesus Christ, the church, his brothers and sisters in the work; it would be treason to consent to the tiniest act of unfaithfulness ... in these moments.
>
> (*Cronica* II, 1972)

and

> To leave the work is a great disgrace ... the founder asserted that he would not give five cents for the soul of one who left.
>
> (Moreno, *El Opus Dei* p.87).

Those who leave Opus Dei are regarded as dead and are not referred to. Those who criticise the organisation are regarded as doing the work of the devil. When journalist Trevor Williams, BBC Radio Ulster, contacted the Opus Dei Head Office in Dublin regarding a proposed radio programme to be broadcast towards the end of 1986, they were not very polite.

He invited them to listen to the tape down the line and offered to record a reply. In response the Opus Dei official questioned Trevor Williams's journalistic integrity and threatened to black him professionally. Opus Dei's tactics for dealing with criticism appears to be to ridicule the critic. Irish freelance journalist, Carol Coulter, tasted some of the Opus Dei back-lash following the publication of her excellent book, *Are Religious Cults Dangerous?* by Mercier Press in 1984. Much to the distaste of Opus Dei official Paul Harman, Ms Coulter had decided to include the movement in her book on religious cults. In Mr Harman's view, Opus Dei's position within the Catholic Church exempted it from the kind of scrutiny to which other groups are subjected by the media. In a letter to the *Irish Times* (28 November, 1984) he claimed that Ms Coulter "had decided not to talk to anyone (in Opus Dei)…instead only to interview and give full credence to certain people who have negative things to say."

He declined Ms Coulter's invitation to reply to the criticisms in her book prior to publication. In Ms Coulter's letter to the *Irish Times* (10 December 1984) she explains :

> What would be of rather more interest to your readers is the information I sought, but did not receive. This was Opus Dei's view on, or refutation of, criticisms made of them by parents, priests and others. Having indeed discovered that people had "negative things to say" about Opus Dei, I offered Mr. Harman the opportunity to reply. This he

declined to do, attempting now to damage my reputation as a journalist instead.

In January 1989, the departing Apostolic Nuncio to Ireland, Archbishop Gaetano Alibrandi, paid an unprecedented tribute to Opus Dei and labelled critics of the organisation "phony liberals." Retiring after twenty years as the Pope's representative in Ireland, he said that his esteem and love for the organisation had grown along with his admiration for the founder, Monsignor Escrivá. He added that the decision by Pope John Paul II to make Opus Dei a "Personal Prelature" had appeared to some "jaundiced eyes" as prejudicial to the diocesan jurisdiction of bishops, but that nothing could be further from the truth. The Archbishop's remarks appeared in *The Sunday Independent* of 8 January 1989, and in the Catholic church magazine, *Intercom*. This was viewed by Opus Dei supporters in Ireland as a major boost to the organisation.

According to Klaus Steigleder, a former numerary in Germany who published an account of his association with Opus Dei in the German magazine *Der Spiegel*: "Their theology stands and falls with the Founder's authority. He is supposed to have concrete knowledge of God's will. This allows them to call continually on an authority that cannot be criticised." Monsignor Escrivá himself declared: "My doctrine is not mine but comes from God and so not a jot or tittle shall be changed." Monsignor Alvaro del Portillo acknowledges: "We are his children; we cannot criticise our father." Paul Harman, official spokesman for Opus Dei in Ireland, puts it much more subtly :

> Catholics who trust the Church's judgement (the Pope) can rest easy ... its aims (Opus Dei) have

nothing to do with the 'new wave religious movements' which have appeared in recent years; and anyone using terminology associated with cults when talking about Opus Dei is unaware of the truth, if not deliberately distorting it.

> (Letters to the Editor, *Irish Independent*,
> 23 July 1987)

Perhaps ironically, it is Opus Dei's militant orthodoxy that has made it so controversial within the Church in the light of the liberalising effects of Vatican II. A senior Jesuit, interviewed for the *New York Times Magazine* (January 8, 1984), described Opus Dei as :

> a throwback to pre-Vatican days. Vatican II brought an end to the old idea that the church is the perfect society, that there could be no criticism. Where are we when orthodoxy again becomes an end in itself ? Where is the room for research, for theological investigation? The idea that human society must be entirely subordinated to the purposes of the church — we have gotten away from this.

Perhaps the most important book of all for Opus Dei members is *The Way*, the organisation's "bible," which consists of 999 maxims written by the founder Monsignor Escrivá. According to *The Way* (Maxim No 936) Opus Dei members should submit themselves to the organisation rather than impose their own opinions on it:

> You have come to the apostolate to submit, to annihilate yourself: not to impose your own personal viewpoint.

Chapter 2

Recruiting Young Souls

> By no means...are parents called upon to abandon
> their Child into the hands of the professionals, be
> they of the Church or the State.
> > Cardinal Silvio Oddie, Prefect for the Vatican's
> > Sacred Congregation for the Clergy

The main purpose of Opus Dei-influenced centres is the recruitment into the movement of those who attend. This is a priority of which members are regularly reminded. The importance of recruitment is summed up in the words of "the Father," Monsignor Escrivá de Balaguer when he said: "We do not have any other aim than the corporate one: proselytism, winning vocations" (*Cronica* V 1963) and "Proselytism in the work is precisely the road, the way to reach sanctity" (*Ibid*).

Discussions about potential recruits take priority in conversations at get-togethers of members. Recruitment is dealt with regularly in the internal newsletters and the weekly "confidence chat" with the spiritual director where each member gives a detailed account of his "apostolate." Members are expected to have at least a handful of friends of whom a number are being worked on actively to join or to "whistle" as it is described in Opus Dei circles. The effort put into recruiting members is tied up very closely with sanctification and the failure

18

to recruit often proves a cause of great anxiety to members. While Monsignor Escrivá publicly stated that Opus Dei's corporate activities are a "disinterested service to humanity" he did admit that the corporate enterprises are dedicated to winning new recruits:

> University residences, universities, publishing houses ... are these ends? NO, and what of the end? Well it is two-fold. On the one hand, personal sanctification. And on the other, to promote the greatest possible number of souls dedicated to God in Opus Dei.
>
> *Cronica* VI, 1963 also VII, 1968

A large number of students come into contact with Opus Dei as residents in one of their university houses around Ireland. Country students embarking on university life for the first time arrive in Dublin, Galway, Limerick or Cork seeking good accommodation. They face a wide choice of hostels, rooms on campus, self-catering flats, bedsitters or shared houses. In a letter to *The Irish Times* on January 22, 1981 by W & G Searson, the following comment was made about these residences:

> Turn to these activities run on a corporate basis. Their reason for existence is characteristically simple: Response to a clear need; the need to provide suitable accommodation and environment for students away from their homes for the first time.

The university residences offer high quality accommodation and for first year students, away from home, it is comforting to be free of worries such as finding a flatmate, tenancy agreements, electricity bills and cooking. The Opus Dei university centres are all based near the main Irish universities UCD, UCG, NIHE, and UCC. They provide single rooms and shared accommodation with separate hostels for men and women. Prices vary from residence to residence, reflecting the different facilities available, but in 1988 the average annual cost was £2,000. Residences like Nullamore for men, on the Dartry Road, Dublin offer high-quality accommodation—catering facilities, study rooms, sports facilities, common rooms and a chapel. During leisure time students are encouraged to involve themselves in areas other than their studies such as Opus Dei spiritual activities. Mass, Confession and Communion are made available on a daily basis.

Only a small percentage of the young people who pass through Opus Dei centres will eventually join the organisation. Because of this the movement needs as wide a base as possible, a large pool of potential recruits. Those who do not join in complete dedication as numeraries may later opt to become supernumeraries or associates. Others may well be counted on for their help as co-operators.

In the active programme of continual recruitment a special type of jargon or code has developed within Opus Dei circles. Those in the movement are described as being in *The Work*. A distinction is drawn between "interesting people" and "wets"—people of no benefit to Opus Dei. The term "whistling" is used to describe someone who has just decided to join the movement. Irish members not sufficiently active in recruitment have been referred to as "goats" by the movement's hierarchy abroad. When a person shows his intention to join by writing a letter to "the Father" asking to become an accepted member he is said to have "whistled." He now becomes the "red letter" and he is expected to bring the next potential recruit quickly to the same stage.

Despite assertions by Opus Dei to the contrary, recruitment is an elaborately structured and carefully directed operation. Over the years successful strategies and effective tactics have been developed. Each new worthwhile contact is recorded on a special form where notes are made concerning his occupation, spiritual life and closeness to the work of Opus Dei. Gradually a picture evolves of this person's psychological and religious characteristics and his ripeness or otherwise for a carefully managed "crisis of vocation"—the crunch time when a potential recruit is finally asked to make his mind up. Details concerning recruiting activities in Ireland are regularly sent to the Opus Dei World Headquarters in Rome for scrutiny. Countries and regions with a poor record are placed under pressure by the top brass in Rome to improve their performance.

As the founder of the movement said

> We must spread out like a fan ... we must open up like a hand and have a group of souls ... dangling from each finger ... and pull ... whoever has reached the calling in turn spreads the invitation. Souls ... are like cherries, you pull one and get two.
> *Cronica* IV, 1971.

Partly because of Opus Dei's Spanish origins, it is chiefly interested in the professional and well-educated classes of society. Seriously committed and active Catholics are of great importance to the movement. While recruiting among people with the appropriate background and personal qualities, good looks are not overlooked. The movement has some interest in recruiting among the working class but in practise this forms a minor part of the work, with one notable exception—the women's section works very hard to recruit associates as servants. The recruitment of teenagers is carried out mainly by teenagers themselves under direction from older numeraries who often provide the finishing touches. The primary aim is to persuade each potential recruit to visit an Opus Dei residence centre, prayer meeting or social get-together.

One such meeting I attended at Nullamore University Residence in 1983 was an enlightening experience. I had been asked to accompany a good friend to the get-together. What struck me most about Nullamore was how beautifully decorated the centre was. According to tradition when you visit a residence centre, the first place you are brought to is the chapel. This is always the most ornately decorated room in the centre, and Nullamore's was quite spectacular. The atmosphere was intensely silent and deeply holy. After a few short prayers in the chapel, I was brought into a large room to meet some other invited guests. It was an atmosphere of great friendliness and I was given an opportunity to talk to other people for a considerable length of time. A large number of those present were members of Opus Dei. Suddenly there was an announcement that a short film was to be shown and a request that the lights be dimmed. It was a lengthy film about Monsignor Escrivá, Opus Dei's founder, and included footage from many of his talks. After the film ended three talks on theological aspects of Opus Dei's spirituality were given by a number of prominent businessmen and academics. This was followed by a light meal in the dining hall. A member of the group invited me back on a number of occasions a few weeks later but I declined the offer. I must admit however, that my initial experience was a very pleasant one.

Opus Dei find that making contact with young people is relatively easy through the schools, youth clubs and residences run by the organisation or rather, as Opus Dei likes to clarify, run by individual members who are free to engage themselves in these activities. These centres provide the members of Opus Dei with a captive audience and ideal surroundings in which to woo new recruits. For numeraries who live in the smaller, more remote hostels where only other numeraries live, making contact with new friends is much more difficult. This problem is overcome by inviting newly-made friends to films, weekend camps, hikes and sporting occasions. The pre-university and catering courses also provide an excellent pool of potential recruits. Unfortunately, for the unsuspecting participants that is, the Opus Dei involvement is not always mentioned in the beginning. For example in the *Sunday Press* of April 17, 1983, an advertisement on the appointments page ran as follows:

> A career in catering and housecraft for girls between fifteen and eighteen years of age beginning on July 1. During the course the general education of the students is continued and human and spiritual values are continually fostered by the directors and those who work with the students.

At no point in the advertisement was it stated that the Crannton Catering and Educational Centre, Dublin is run by Opus Dei members.

Opus Dei university undergraduates work very hard

to make contact with other university students, inviting them along to lectures and seminars given in the houses of Opus Dei. Members are to be seen in the foyers of university chaplaincies after Mass attempting to win the friendship of other undergraduates, especially those in their first term at university. These people are invited to evenings of recollection, meditation and benediction in the Oratory of Opus Dei houses followed by a get-together for the visitors. This is regarded as a very important occasion for making new contacts in the right atmosphere.

> Once the benediction is over the fellows naturally spread out through the whole house ... and it is a wonderful opportunity to study them.
>
> The Founder, *Cronica* II 1963

Monsignor Escrivá constantly encouraged members to exercise a "holy audacity" and a "holy coercion" in the apostolate to recruit boldly and openly.

Opus Dei members are trained to present the best possible impression during those first encounters with outsiders. One's profession is seen as a hook with the bait of excellent prestige. According to the founder :

> Each morning, when we go out early to work ... among other things that occupy our thoughts there will be certain targets for proselytism, precisely determined targets. They demand a spirit of sacrifice until they become a reality lived day after day.
>
> *Cronica* VII 1969

In Opus Dei it is firmly believed that an expensively appointed house in the best part of the city, decorated in a secular style and immaculately clean, will impress visitors very much. For example, some of the Irish residence centres are situated in places like Monkstown, Milltown, Dalkey, Donnybrook—all top-class south Dublin areas. For the very same reason Opus Dei will introduce potential recruits to its more impressive looking members.

However, much of this recruitment effort can be very sincere because, within the movement at different levels, there are thoroughly genuine Roman Catholics with a firm religious conviction and dedication to the church.

When a new group of potential recruits is brought to a get-together, the whole atmosphere of the residence changes. It echoes with laughter, macho behaviour and good humoured raillery, all intended to delight the visitors. Very often this is not consciously insincere behaviour. Members slip into it naturally and often it is a relief valve for them. Opus Dei people are astonished at and react strongly to the suggestion that there is any dishonesty in putting on such a show to win vocations for the work of God. They are horrified at any suggestion that they are instrumentalising their friendships with people:

> Did not the founder repeat again and again that theirs was an apostolate of friendship and confidence and what they were doing was the highest form of friendship.
>
> (M. Moreno, *El Opus Dei*, p. 128)

> It is necessary to seek and foster these relationships ... not to 'instrumentalise' friendship as a tactic for social penetration. With holy shrewdness, little by little, but constantly without

haste and without pausing ... you must use everything because everything is a means of apostolate.

The Founder, *Cronica* I, 1967

The constitution of Opus Dei requires that candidates for numerary membership of the organisation should have academic degrees or at least be in preparation for one (Constitution Article No. 35). Those with physical disabilities are not accepted for membership. Opus Dei however has no qualms about recruiting those engaged to be married or already married. The organisation prides itself on its ability to win recruits despite alliances of that sort. The clergy of Opus Dei organise meditations, weekend retreats and seminars for diocesan priests again with the primary purpose of attracting them to the movement. Opus Dei is interested in converting Protestants and those of other religious persuasions—but always with a view to persuading them to join *The Work* at a later stage. Anyone who has not been a member of Opus Dei, or of a similar organisation, can hardly imagine the singleness of purpose involved in turning every possible contact with the outside world to the benefit of the movement.

The numerary, supernumerary, associate or priest designated to work on a potential recruit is supposed to have a weekly chat and telephone him or her regularly. If that person is ill he will be visited. On his birthday he may receive an elaborate card covered in amusing remarks by the members of his local Opus Dei centre. Spanish members are particularly demonstrative in their affection. Traditional works of mercy, such as visiting the sick, are sometimes used as a means to persuade potential recruits to accompany members of Opus Dei in visiting the poor and sick in hospital or at home. Importance is placed on getting the person to pay his own bus fare if public transport is being used. A long route is chosen if possible so that the member appointed to "work on" him has time to lead the conversation around to Opus Dei and to involve him in some way. When a group of members go on a trip with "potentials," it is arranged so that each "potential" is appointed a "friend" and the priest can have time to take him aside for a private chat during which he is pushed a little further down the road of recruitment.

Those invited at minimal expense to Opus Dei's conference of Catholic students in Rome each Easter, with the prospect of an audience with the Pope, are often unaware that they are actually participating in Opus Dei's annual pilgrimage from all over the world to the tomb of the founder. One important aspect of the trip is the visit to the head of the movement in Rome who is said to have quasi-sacramental power to make people who see him join Opus Dei soon afterwards. Next in importance is a visit to Opus Dei's main international seminary where the numeraries from each country will do everything in their power to persuade the visitor to join while in Rome—or at least promise to receive spiritual direction from the Opus Dei priest when he or she returns home. Finally, Opus Dei draws extra benefit from the gathering by organising a mass audience with the Pope. The group is presented to His Holiness as if all those attending were members or at least ardent sympathisers with Opus Dei, and, of course, fully loyal to the Papacy.

The groups of young people attached to Opus Dei clubs are regarded as the seed-bed of its vocations. Prayer, self-mortification and organised activities are used to draw this circle closer and closer into the movement. The main techniques used to achieve this are: the enthusiastic projection of a highly attractive image of Opus Dei which secures loyalty and admiration and counters criticism (*The Way*, Nos. 661, 944, 945); winning the trust, affection and admiration of the recruit for the designated member working on him and meeting him weekly for a personal chat and a meditation on *The Way*; establishing regular spiritual direction and confession with an Opus Dei priest; the encouragement of regular religious practices and a deepening of religious faith; the reading of the religious publications of Opus Dei and attendance at the weekly "circle" meditations, monthly and yearly retreats.

> In entrusting us with this work God has confided these souls, the youth, the hope of the work to us... these youngsters that God himself has placed in our hands deserve all our concern, all our affection. May there be a large nursery.
>
> *Cronica* VII 1962

> (the role) of the girls who come to the St. Raphael (recruiting) circle... is that of disciples who come to listen to a teacher. They do not argue. Without the nuisance of a chorus of spectators it is easy to help them.
>
> *Cronica* VII,1965

Possibly the single most important device employed by the movement to nourish its seed-bed of vocations is the weekly "circle." These organised group chats are given to teenagers, university undergraduates and to older professional people. Those who go along for the first time rarely know that the person who invited them was the member appointed to work on them. The latter goes along to the circle as if he were just another interested attendant, and so do most of the numeraries in the house. The visitor finds himself in an atmosphere of rapt attention to the words of the speaker giving the address. During the talk the speakers might stress: the importance of study and the excellent study facilities available in that house; the importance of having a plan of life which includes regular spiritual practices and the obvious need for a spiritual guide to carry it out; that there happens to be in the house a priest who is also a trained professional man, and he will be only too willing to provide basic Christian guidance; that the trouble with some priests today is they have strayed from the traditional teachings of the Church and are spreading false doctrine; fortunately the priest of the house is not like that, he can be trusted absolutely and offers authentic Church teaching.

Sometimes during the circle there is a break during which a secret collection bag is circulated to help the running of the house. When the talk is over most numeraries hang around to speak to the visitors who find themselves in the centre of a smiling, humorous and affectionate group. A visitor may be invited to a game of football or a weekend trip. The priest of the house may affectionately call the guest aside and encourage him to tell personal things about himself and suggest having a chat with him soon again. The numerary working on him will be the hero of the moment. The only individual rewards in Opus Dei are approval and promotion, and the highest regard is reserved for those who win many recruits. As the visitor being worked on comes to the circle more frequently he learns from his new friends about the marvels of *The Work*; how fantastic it is; how it is made up of ordinary laymen and women like himself living their lives in the midst of the world. Some of them are married. They did not change their professions when called to join God in Opus Dei. They are very brilliant professionals, company directors, ministers, top rank businessmen—all sanctifying the world from within with the same freedoms, ambitions and responsibilities as everyone else.

The skill in timing the "crisis of vocation" and guiding someone through it to a successful outcome is regarded as the highest form of apostolic art in Opus Dei (*The Way* No. 803). To provoke it the numerary working on the individual involved must obtain the consent of the director of the house, who discusses the matter in a local council attended by the Opus Dei priest responsible for that area. The whole process is carefully engineered. It involves frequent, long and intense conversa with the person to be recruited, in which every possible device of human and religious persuasion is employed to convince him that God is calling him to join Opus Dei now—and that not to do so is to turn his back on God and seriously risk eternal damnation (*Catholic Pictorial* November 29 1981, p.14). The person about to "whistle" can often feel under tremendous emotional, moral and religious pressure, which is sometimes accompanied by fear.

> People become frightened. They are surprised at our eagerness to bring other souls to God to serve him.
>
> (The Founder, *Cronica* IV, 1971)

Opus Dei is quite determined about provoking a crisis of vocation when it believes someone is ready for it. The imminence of final examinations or the pleas of parents will not cause it to relent. The mother of a young assistant numerary in Dublin has described to the author how some years ago her daughter, who was then being trained in one of the Opus Dei-run catering schools, telephoned her in tears saying she was unhappy and wished to return home. Her mother spoke to the directress who explained that her daughter was merely worried about examinations and eventually she was persuaded to stay on at the school. The girl's mother now bitterly regrets her decision, having discovered that her daughter was then being pressed to join Opus Dei, which she did soon afterwards. She has subsequently become completely alienated from her daughter.

Opus Dei has found it increasingly difficult to persuade university graduates to "whistle" so it now concentrates more heavily on teenagers with its recruitment programme directed at clubs and schools. Adverse publicity about the movement and allegations that its methods of operation are similar to those of religious cults have badly hampered their recruitment drive. A *Magill* magazine investigation published in May 1983 was a major blow to the organisation. It was written by Maurice Roche, a former teacher at the Rockbrook National Boys' School in Rathfarnham where members of Opus Dei are involved in the running of the school. A series of *Live Line* programmes on Opus Dei's Irish activities broadcast on RTE Radio at the end of 1986 also gave voice to widespread concern. Parents complained bitterly that they were not involved in their sons' or daughters' decision to join the movement. Some broke down on the live broadcast in fits of sadness and despair. Others spoke angrily of their dislike of the organisation's activities.

Those who decide to join Opus Dei are not always aware of the implications of membership and the strict guidelines imposed on numeraries and assistant numeraries. The founder frequently stated how each new vocation is a gentle flame which must be protected, otherwise it will easily be extinguished. This protection is extended to the period immediately before new members "whistle."

> In this period of transition be prudent in imposing and even manifesting the obligations which our people have.
>
> (*Cronica* II, 1963.)

Numeraries and associates are not always told that once they have joined their letters may be read, or that they will be required to take the *discipline* and wear the *cilis*; that permission from the director may be required for them to read a particular book or watch a television programme; that permission may also be required for them to visit their parents or friends. Discos, parties and social occasions are seen as a potential threat or source of temptation to members and so these are forbidden without prior permission. Other innumerable commitments and "family customs" in Opus Dei are only discovered after a period of time. How then does this match up to the claim that Opus Dei members live as ordinary lay people in the midst of the world?

It is apparent that the often questionable practical directives applied by Opus Dei are cushioned by a background of noble generalities. These generalities are often sharply incompatible with the specific directives. For example : "Force them to come in, push them" and "It is perfectly compatible with the most delicate respect for freedom of souls." (The Founder, *Cronica* IV, 1971).

Members of Opus Dei often genuinely fail to see the incongruity of this, precisely because the founder's admirable generalities about freedom, joy, sincerity, openness and so forth are never translated into practical directives—while directives about coercion, manipulation, secrecy and so on are never expressed as generalities. These specifics are avoided and refuted. In the public defence of Opus Dei, members have been trained to recall only the founder's impeccable generalities, never his practical directives. This explains their often sincere outrage at general accusations of totalitarianism, secrecy or manipulation (Letters to the *Irish Press* and *Irish Times*, 21—31 January, 1981). It is also very significant that recruitment, which according to the founder is the corporate aim of Opus Dei, is not mentioned specifically in its constitutions. Outsiders who imagine that those who join Opus Dei are either social misfits, sub-intelligent or so weak as persons that they need to surrender their will to an institution, are unaware of certain key factors in the methods of recruitment: the cultivation and attraction of an intense religious faith centred on Opus Dei (backed by the Church); the provision of a total environment; the high-pressure techniques employed and the picture of life within the organisation painted to catechumens. The techniques used to gain recruits and to secure their continued allegiance are equally powerful and involve an equally vast expenditure of time, resources and effort. For Opus Dei, the Catholic Church provides an enormous pool of potential recruits. Its approval by the Roman Curia and the Pope—an approval which the organisation tirelessly publicises—gives it a far easier access to recruits and far greater respectability than any other religious or lay organisation in the world. Respectability and recognition aside, Opus Dei's methods of recruitment and operation in this country are a cause of considerable anxiety and dismay among lay Catholics and non-Catholics alike.

Chapter 3

In the Beginning...

In order to understand the whole concept of Opus Dei, one has to examine closely the heart and mind of its founder, Father Josemaría Escrivá de Balaguer, born in Barbastro in the northern Spanish province of Huesa on 9 January, 1902. Opus Dei is distinctly marked by its Spanish origins and the organisation grew out of various social, political and religious upheavals and traditions of Escrivá's time.

In Spain, the two forces that had played a major role in shaping the modern world, the Reformation and the French Revolution, were seen as hostile and evil. Opus Dei developed at a time when there was bitter rivalry between Catholics and anti-clerical liberals. Opus Dei, founded by Fr Escrivá in 1928, was to be the movement which would protect the traditional teaching of the Roman Catholic Church for both lay and religious during a time when Catholics were seen as targets for growing revolutionary anger. The problems were more clearly evident during the Spanish Civil War (1936-39) which Fr Escrivá viewed as a crusade against the evils of godlessness, materialism, decadence and what he saw as the black plague of communism.

Escrivá's parents, Dolores and Don José, married in 1898 and lived in Barbastro where Dolores had grown up. All but one of their six children were born at home, including Josemaría. Dona Dolores had the assistance of a cook, a maid and a nanny to look after the house while a manservant was employed to do the heavy work. It was she who instilled in her children a very strong Christian outlook on life. In the intensely religious atmosphere of the Escrivá home young Josemaría learned to pray and say the Rosary every day. Each Saturday the family visited a nearby church with other families to attend lengthy religious services. By the time Josemaría made his First Holy Communion, he was already studying at a school run by a religious order, the Piarists, in Barbastro.

Over the years, the family suffered successive blows with the childhood deaths of three daughters. Rosario, the youngest, was the first to die before she was one year old; Dolores died when she was five and Chon died shortly after her eighth birthday.

When Chon died, Josemaría was eleven years old and his eldest sister Carmen was barely fourteen. Both were deeply affected by the tragic events and Josemaría even began to say that his turn was next since his sisters had all died in ascending order from the youngest upwards.

Towards the end of 1913, the textile business of Josemaría's father, Don José, was close to ruin. As a result the family had to get rid of the cook, the maid and the rest of the servants. The nanny had already been let go after Chon died. In 1915 the Escrivás were forced to sell the house which had been a home to them for over fifteen years. Today, an educational centre run by Opus Dei occupies the site of the Escrivá family home.

The family moved on to the small north-central Spanish city of Logrono, where Don José had found some work. Life was difficult during the first few months in Logrono as the Escrivá family hardly knew anyone there. Josemaría continued his studies in the nearby Logrono

Institute, in literary composition, ethics and law. The pupils usually went to the Institute in the morning until lunchtime. In the afternoons they attended religious classes and long periods of study, at one of two tutorial schools in the area. Josemaría went to St Anthony's College which was run by laymen although it had a residential spiritual director. Those wishing to join the priesthood in those days usually entered the seminary when they reached the age of ten. Josemaría had never thought the priesthood was for him but later changed his mind when he felt God wanted something special from him. This is how he described his feelings:

> There comes to my mind so many manifestations of God's love during my adolescent years, when I sensed that our Lord wanted something of me. Ordinary events and happenings, seemingly without significance, yet he used them to plant within my soul a divine restlessness ... they stirred and led me to daily communion, purification, confession and penance.

Until this time, Josemaría had thought of becoming an architect. When he reached his decision to join the priesthood he decided to tell his father. It was the only time he saw his father cry. Don José had other plans for his son but decided not to prevent him from entering the priesthood.

In October 1918, at the age of sixteen, Josemaría commenced his studies for the priesthood in the seminary of Logrono. He was a day student, supplementing his training at home with two priests as his tutors. His only brother, Santiago, was born the following year. In September 1920 Josemaría transferred to the seminary of St Francis de Paula in Saragossa and found himself away from home for the first time in his life. Just months before he was ordained a priest in 1925, Josemaría's father died. Don José had always been counting on Josemaría to care for the family when he died and so the family decided to move to Saragossa to be with Josemaría.

In Saragossa, Josemaría began a way of life as a young seminarian very different to anything he had previously experienced. It was a life divided between the seminary and studies at the local university to obtain a civil law degree. Life in the seminary was regimented. In the morning Josemaría meditated for half an hour before morning Mass. Following early breakfast he left for classes at the Pontifical University in double file with other seminarians, accompanied by a superior. After early afternoon dinner, he returned to classes, followed by periods of recreation, study and Rosary. In the evening he said prayers with the other seminarians and listened to religious talks. If he wished to go for a walk, it was a rule that he was always accompanied by another student.

Josemaría found life in the seminary very difficult. It was hard for him to settle into the new way of life. The atmosphere of the seminary was so different to what he had found at St Anthony's College in Logrono. Many of the students in the seminary at Saragossa disliked Josemaría intensely. He was always perfectly dressed and the epitome of good manners. Josemaría washed daily from head to foot, something which the other seminarians did not do. He appeared aloof, pensive and introverted and did not mix well. However his outlook on life endeared him very much to his superiors, so much so that he was appointed superior (prefect) of the seminary in 1922 and assigned a personal attendant. His relationship with his fellow students deteriorated further with this appointment. They were particularly incensed when the Archbishop of Saragossa, Cardinal Soldevila called to the seminary one day and singled Josemaría out in front of the others as an outstanding student.

It is reported that the Cardinal would enquire of Josemaría as to how his studies were coming along, often adding "come and see me when you have the time." The superiors at the seminary were always chosen from among the more promising and pious students. As one of the superiors, Josemaría was responsible for directing studies, seeing that discipline and rules were observed, and accompanying the other pupils when they went out to class, for a walk or on trips. Although the superiors were seminarians as well, by rule they had to be obeyed and respected. Josemaría was given special privileges. He had a servant and a single room which was larger than the rest.

On 28 March 1925 Josemaría received Holy Orders and decided to live with his family. In Spain, where presbyteries are scarce, most priests live with members of their family. With the permission of Saragossa's Archbishop in May 1927, Fr Escrivá moved with his family to Madrid—the only city in Spain at that time where he could obtain a doctorate in civil law. Madrid was bustling with nearly one million people, many of them recent arrivals from the farms and shantytowns which encirlced the city. Fr Escrivá continued his work, preaching, looking after community needs of his parishioners and working on his doctorate in the University of Madrid.

The day which was to change his life, 2 October, 1928, found him at a retreat at a residence of the Missionaries of St Vincent de Paul in Madrid. While studying some papers in his room, Fr Escrivá claimed that he was suddenly overcome by what he saw was "Opus Dei as God wanted it to be, projected through the centuries." He always refused to go into the details of what happened that day, insisting that Opus Dei belonged to God and that he did not wish to steal any of His glory. Fr Escrivá said it was on that date that he learned with "crystal clarity that he, then only a 26 - year old priest, virtuallly unknown, was to be God's chosen instrument to establish Opus Dei on earth." He partially explained his vision of Opus Dei in an interview with the *New York Times* in 1966:

> The spirit of Opus Dei reflects the marvellous reality that any honest and worthwhile work can be converted into a divine occupation. In God's service, there are no second class jobs; all of them are important. To love and serve God, there is no need to do anything strange or extraordinary. Christ bids all without exception to be perfect as His heavenly Father is perfect. Sanctity, for the vast majority of people, implies sanctifying their work, sanctifying themselves in it, and sanctifying others through it. Thus they can encounter God in the course of their daily lives.

Early members of Opus Dei were amazed at Fr Escrivá's vision, at the scope and detail of his plan and at what they saw as a new way for lay people to devote their daily work to God. Opus Dei represented a novelty within the Church's life but in some ways also a distinct threat. Fr Escrivá believed that he had invented, with divine inspiration, something wholly new in Catholic spirituality: the idea that all are called to holiness within the circumstances of their lay life and their secular calling. However, many argued that sodalities, third orders, and oblates had all been founded on the assumption that holiness and sanctity was for everyone and could be lived in the world. They believed the Opus Dei claim to originality was incorrect and a distortion of history. Preaching about his vision on 2 October, 1962, Fr Escrivá said :

> From that moment on (his claimed inspiration from God) I never had any tranquility and I began to work, reluctantly, because I did not like the idea of being the founder of anything. But I began to work, to move, to do, to lay the foundations.

He was later to say :

> The Lord has been tutoring me from the beginning of the work, and I cannot but sing His praises and fight to fulfil His will, because if I didn't, the salvation of my soul would be at stake.

In the late '20s and '30s, besides his work as Opus Dei's founder, Fr Escrivá served as a chaplain to a charitable organisation known as the Foundation for the Sick. It had been started in Madrid by a group of Catholic women. His work involved visits to public hospitals which were overcrowded and had poor facilities. The atmosphere of anti-clericalism at the time very often led patients to view any priest with hostililty. But Fr Escrivá would not be deterred. Everywhere he went he kept on the lookout for potential recruits who would commit themselves to Opus Dei. Sick people in hospital, some critically ill, were easy recruits. Fr Escrivá later claimed that Opus Dei was born among the poor and sick of Madrid's hospitals.

Strangely, Fr Escrivá had limited himself to seeking male recruits for Opus Dei. But in 1930 he decided that there was no reason why women could not be admitted, as he believed they were also called to the same spiritual programme. In that year he laid the foundation for the women's section of Opus Dei.

There were major difficulties, however. At that time women enjoyed very little freedom and it was not customary for them to attend a university or enter professions. They had a traditional place in Spanish society, a servile role in the home. Many of Fr Escrivá's followers abandoned him because of his plan to recruit women. It was a minor setback.

In January 1933, the Opus Dei founder began a series of weekly classes in practical Christian living for college students in Madrid. It was to be the first ever recruiting course for Opus Dei. But only three people came to the first class. These pupils were encouraged to bring others and so within a number of years Fr Escrivá was giving several classes every day. The pupils were sent out to teach catechism to the poor people of the city on Sunday mornings. To complement his classes, Fr Escrivá wrote and published a number of books containing points for meditation as a guide to his growing number of followers. His most famous book, *Spiritual Considerations*, was published in 1934. Five years later it was extended and reissued as *The Way*—what Opus Dei today view as the founder's classic work and the organisation's rule book.

Opus Dei became more discreet about its operations in the early 1930s. When the Republic was proclaimed in Spain in 1931, the Ministry for Justice published a statement heavily criticising the wealth of the Catholic Church. As a direct result, some churches were burned and convents destroyed. The Church Rule of 1933 ordered the separation of Church and State, and withdrew the influence of the Church from many schools. Against this backdrop Opus Dei developed a shyness about open publicity and Fr Escrivá was forced to work in secret. He wrote at the time : "The confidentiality of the apostolate is evident, not without reason." The Spain of Fr Escrivá's time still held on to medieval Catholicism that was filled with secrecy, mystery and zeal. It was an honoured religious tradition to flog oneself in public, something which Opus Dei members today perform in private. Fr Escrivá's aim was to re-channel the zeal of the '30s into purifying the church.

Between 1918 and 1923 serious social and industrial unrest disrupted the life of Spain. During that period the country had twelve governments but none was able to introduce long-term reforms to bring stability to the country. In 1923 General Primo de Rivera seized power with the help of the army and proclaimed a military dictatorship. During Rivera's rule some social reforms were initiated. However, by 1928 serious rioting began to take place throughout Spain and a radical socialist party fought to end Rivera's rule and the Spanish monarchy with which it was associated. Rivera decided to resign. In 1934 the conservative opposition won the Spanish elections and tried to undo the reforms of the previous years under the liberal and socialist government. The actions of the conservatives had the effect of uniting all the radical groups—the republicans, socialists and communists—who together formed a "Popular Front" which won the election of 1936. The new Prime Minister Anza brought in a written constitution which halted government payments to priests, suspended religious education and abolished a number of monastic orders. This infuriated Fr Escrivá and his Opus Dei followers who saw their organisation as being under threat.

Up to 1933, Fr Escrivá carried out his work in all kinds of places and he had a growing number of followers. He was determined, despite the political atmosphere, to establish a central headquarters for Opus Dei. As a result, the DYA (*Dios y Audacia*—God and Daring) Opus Dei Academy was opened in late 1933 in a small rented apartment in Madrid. It was a cultural and educational centre not unlike the present Opus Dei university residence centes throughout the world. In the heated political atmosphere of the time, many of the Opus Dei followers were against Fr Escrivá's plans to open such a centre as they felt it would draw direct attention to the organisation.

When the Spanish Civil War broke out in 1936 and especially with the outbreak of the Second World War in 1939, Fr Escrivá had to postpone the expansion of Opus Dei. During the Civil War, Fr Escrivá was forced to remain in his mother's house. The organisation went further underground. Priests in Madrid at the time had to hide or leave themselves open to assassination by a street patrol. These were days and months of total confusion. During the Civil War 184 secular priests, 2,365 religious and 283 nuns met their deaths. Rumours abounded that Fr Escrivá had also been killed. In order to survive in the tense atmosphere, Opus Dei learned to be cunning: how to hide and camouflage itself; to use false papers and operate in secret. Fr Escrivá introduced strict laws of discipline, control and censorship to protect the movement. Religious persecution continued through the Civil War with the burning of convents and churches. Catholic schools were banned. Quite often, anti-clerical sentiments ran wild, abetted by the authorities. Self-proclaimed militias sprang up to hunt down priests with the result that thirty per cent of the priests in Madrid were assassinated.

During the winter and spring of 1936-37 Fr Escrivá took refuge in a small psychiatric hospital on the outskirts of the capital. From here he re-established contact with some of the dispersed members of Opus Dei. He found a somewhat better arrangement in the home of the Honduran Consul General which enjoyed a precarious diplomatic immunity. This lasted from March to August 1937. After thirteen months of war and with no end in sight, he decided to leave the relative safety of the Honduran Consul with documentation accrediting him as an employee of the consulate, in an effort to escape to the other side of Spain. There, without the threat of religious persecution, he could continue his plans for Opus Dei. With the aid of some friends Fr Escrivá managed to escape to the nationalist region of Spain where Catholics were much safer.

The long and dangerous trip lasted weeks but finally the exhausted group reached Andorra on 2 December, 1937 and from there proceeded to France, Lourdes and into nationalist Spain. In his escape to the other side, Fr Escrivá had left behind, mostly in Madrid, some members of Opus Dei and his mother, sister and brother. He was keen to let them know of his whereabouts and keep their hopes alive. However, there was no exchange of mail between Spain's warring sides. By mid-December Fr Escrivá found himself a guest of the bishop of Pamplona in northern Spain. From there he sent mail to a friend in southern France, who forwarded letters bound for Madrid, omitting all religious references in order to avoid censorship of the letter by the authorities. This was the only way of maintaining contact with his family and friends in Opus Dei.

The end of the Civil War was marked by the taking of

Madrid by the Nationalists on 28 March, 1939. That day Fr Escrivá returned to the capital to begin the reconstruction of the Opus Dei movement. Within months a new residence hall was opened in Madrid. The founder travelled to different Spanish cities each weekend in search of young recruits.

Vocations were springing up. A small centre was opened in Valencia marking the start of the expansion outside of the capital. The first women's branch of Opus Dei opened in 1942 in a quiet residential neighbourhood in Madrid. Until 1944, Fr Escrivá was the only Opus Dei priest. However in that year three veteran members of the work were studying for the priesthood and soon to be ordained. They were: José Luis Múzquiz, who helped start Opus Dei in America in 1949; José Maria Hernández de Garnica, who worked in many European countries and Alvaro del Portillo, the current President General of Opus Dei. Fr Escriva was to comment many times that the first ordination of priests, who were also members of Opus Dei (a section called the Sacredotal Society of the Holy Cross) had caused him "at the same time great joy and sadness." He explained :

> I love the lay condition of our work so much that it really hurt me to make them clerics; yet on the other hand, the need for priests was so clear that it had to be pleasing to God that these sons of mine should be ordained priests.

It was always the founder's wish that Opus Dei find a place within the legal framework of the Roman Catholic Church. After the civil war the time had arrived to open a path for Opus Dei in the field of canon law. He believed Opus Dei was unlike any of the other organisations which existed in the church. Its members neither wished to be nor could be "religious" like those who seek holiness by separating themselves from the world. The full apostolic vocation of Opus Dei distinguished it from other confraternities and pious unions which were recognised by the Code of Canon Law. He was convinced that with the help of his legal expertise Opus Dei could obtain legal recognition from the Vatican as a part of the Roman Catholic Church. The apostolic phenomenon had to precede the legal framework. He also knew that Opus Dei could never succeed if it were to cut itself off from the ecclesiastical hierarchy. In the years to follow, Opus Dei was viewed by many within the Roman Curia with great suspicion. Some believed Fr Escrivá to be a saint, others a heretic.

When people stepped up attacks against Opus Dei and its founder, the Bishop of Madrid acted quickly by giving the movement an approval in writing with the aim of mitigating the war of words. Opus Dei began to spread into new cities—Valencia, Barcelona, Saragossa, Valladolid, Seville—and this growth made it all the more urgent to obtain written legal recognition of Opus Dei from the Vatican.

A group of Opus Dei members had begun their studies with a view to being ordained to the priesthood; it was important to solve the points of law which their ordination would pose. In view of these and other reasons Papal approval was vital. In February 1946, Don Alvaro del Portillo was sent to Rome to place before the Vatican documents on Opus Dei which had been prepared by Fr Escrivá. The reception was mixed. Soon afterwards Don Alvaro wrote to the founder saying that he would have to come to Rome himself to try and make some headway because progress seemed impossible.

Why Fr Escrivá did not visit Rome in the first instance himself has not been explained. Perhaps he knew there would be a cold reception. Because of the impasse, Fr Escrivá decided to go to Rome. He brought together the General Council of Opus Dei and told them what he had decided. In 1961 he spoke of the difficulties:

> To the world and the Church, the work seemed a novelty. And the juridicial solutions I was looking for, an impossiblity. But I couldn't wait for things to become possible. A distinguished member of the Roman Curia told us "you have come a century too soon". Nevertheless, we had to try the impossible. I was being urged by the thousands of souls who were committing themselves to God in his work.

By 1945 nine major Spanish cities had Opus Dei centres alongside their universities. Fr Escrivá sent some of his more experienced members to recruit members in Portugal, England and Italy. Later the movement spread to France, Germany and Ireland. Opus Dei was beginning to develop internationally; it needed more than ever the approval of the Holy See.

Fr Escrivá spent most of the second half of 1946 in Rome dealing with Vatical officials. The movement was welcomed by Monsignor Giovanni Montini the Vatican's Under Secretary of State (later to become Pope Paul IV). Others were sceptical about finding an adequate place for Opus Dei within the Church's structure. In spite of the opposition, Fr Escrivá returned to Madrid on August 31 with an "approval of aims" from Pope Pius XII, a document which the Holy See had not issued for over a century. During the next three years Opus Dei was to receive various Holy See approvals and Fr Escrivá was named Monsignor by Pope Pius. In 1947 the Holy See recognised Opus Dei as a "secular institute" and this provided the basis for complete Vatican approval which was granted on June 16, 1950.

But Monsignor Escrivá was dissatisfied even with the status of "secular institute."

He believed there were too many other movements recognised as secular institutes. He was looking for a new status to give Opus Dei a stamp of originality and greater importance. In order for this new move to succeed some major, but subtle changes were made. Two standard Opus Dei works, *Secular Institutes and Opus Dei* and *Priests of Opus Dei* written by Julian Herranz, were quietly withdrawn from circulation in the early 1960s. Members carefully examined back issues of the organisation's internal magazines, *Cronica* and *Obras*, removing offending pages and substituting newly approved terminology. Changes in the constitution were made: "oblates" became "associates," "superiors" became "spiritual directors" and the "secular institute" became an "association."

The whole aim was to avoid giving any impression that Opus Dei resembled a religious order or a secular institute. One of the most important changes was in the constitution Article No. 523 regarding the notion of vows. These were no longer to be taken but would be replaced by a "contractual bond," a specific written agreement between the organisation and intending member outlining mutual obligations. It was very much a cosmetic exercise. Full members of Opus Dei today still commit themselves to living according to the spirit of the founder, a life of poverty, chastity and obedience.

Monsignor Escrivá always claimed—as Opus Dei does today—that he had invented something new in Cahtolic spirituality. He believed this novel view of his was confirmed by the Conciliar Constitution, *Lumen Gentium*, (the Second Vatican Council's Constitution on the Church), which speaks of the universal call to holiness and the importance of the laity in the life of the Church. It was Vatican II that opened the door for the option of "personal prelature." However, both Pope John XXIII and Paul VI had their reservations about Opus Dei and played for time. They did not share Escrivá's high estimation of the movement. Although Monsignor Escrivá never criticised Popes publicly, in private he did not like John XXIII because he considered him undistinguished, of peasant origins, and he detested his views on many subjects. He was more supportive of Paul VI but to Monsignor Escrivá the Pontiff was presiding over the disintegration of the Church.

In many ways, Vatican II was only useful to Opus Dei in that it could and did, improve the status of Opus Dei. In the aftermath of the Council, Monsignor Escrivá felt a painful solicitude for the whole Church. As a result of this, Bibles published after 1962 were considered "tendentious" by Opus Dei; Catholic newspapers were not admitted into Opus Dei houses; books were censored and carefully vetted; post-Conciliar theology was (and is) regarded with suspicion. Opus Dei was to become the advance guard of sanctified and purified worldliness.

As the organisation grew and the financial difficulties caused by this expansion multiplied, Monsignor Escrivá stressed that neither Opus Dei nor its members needed money "because each one works at his professional task and more than earns his keep. But as regards our corporate works, the more we are helped the better we can serve souls." The corporate works referred to, were to include educational institutions, schools for professional development and advancement, youth clubs, university residences and publications. As Opus Dei developed, so too did its finances and influence in social affairs. Accusations of alleged political interests followed when on one occasion a member of the Roman Curia congratulated Monsignor Escrivá on the appointment of a member of Opus Dei, Alberto Ullastres, as a Minister in the Spanish Government. The founder gave the following reply: "What do I care if he is a Minister or a road sweeper. What I care about is that he should sanctify himself in his work."

Monsignor Escrivá believed that Opus Dei was born to play a world-wide role and so it was vital to be close to the Church's world-wide leader.

"We have come to serve the Church and the Church wishes to be served," explained Monsignor Escrivá and with that utterance Opus Dei established its world-wide headquarters in Rome at the end of the 1940s in what has become a major complex of buildings on the Bruno Buzzi. The headquarters were to house the Roman College of the Holy Cross for men, and the Roman College of Saint Mary for women. Students were sent to Rome from various countries to be educated in the Opus Dei message. After several years in Rome these men and women returned to their native lands, or to a new one, to recruit for Opus Dei.

Throughout the 'fifties and 'sixties Opus Dei members visited a host of new countries. In the media, the movement was often referred to as "Octopus Dei" due to the vigour and extent of its recruitment activities. Following Vatican II, and ten years before his death, Monsignor Escrivá worked hard on the expansion of the movement and he travelled widely giving talks and developing the membership. Many of these talks were question and answer type gatherings where he would speak to large crowds and offer advice on spiritual matters. Much of his time was spent tending the consolidation of Opus Dei in Rome and dealing with the Vatican. Monsignor Escrivá made it his business to cultivate Karol Wojtyla (later Pope John Paul II) because of his ultra conservative views on social issues, uncomprimising anti-communism and papal absolutism. When John Paul I died after just 33 days in office, Opus Dei used its considerable power to help swing support for the Polish Cardinal.

Monsignor Escrivá was an obsessive man in the sense that all his time and efforts were devoted to the success and growth of Opus Dei. He was relentlessly conservative in Church matters as he was in political questions. He spoke of Opus Dei as "a pure, firm current which will be recognised once the turbulent waters die down and the river returns to its true bed." Put another way—when the crisis of the post-Conciliar church has blown itself out, Opus Dei will appear to all as the guardian of tradition. Monsignor Escrivá died in Rome on June 26, 1975 in the room where he worked. His body lies in the Crypt of the Oratory of Our Lady of Peace in the Opus Dei Rome headquarters and prayers are constantly said there. He did not live to hear the celebrated announcement on November 27, 1982 that granted Opus Dei the position of "personal prelature."

With this declaration the movement shifted from the care of the Congregation for Religious and Secular Institutes to that of the Congregation of Bishops which appoints bishops. It was a great triumph for Opus Dei, seen by supporters as vindicating the founder's claim to originality. Opus Dei was now a sort of quasi-diocese covering, in principal, the whole world and not defined by territory. It was to become a world-wide diocese made up of both priests and laity but answerable directly only to the Pope and the President General. This new status brought Opus Dei out of the control of the local clergy and bishops. In making the announcement, Cardinal Sebastino Baggio of the Congregation of Bishops said that although the majority of those consulted in the Vatican were in favour of this new status, "not a few had made observations or requests for clarification." He gave no further explanation as to what he meant.

The formal process for the beatification and canonisation of the founder was opened in Rome in 1981 supported by 69 cardinals and 1,300 bishops. Considering Pope John Paul's declared support for Opus Dei it may not be long before Monsignor Escrivá is made a saint. However, in recent years, damaging allegations against Opus Dei have slowed up the process of Escrivá's canonisation. The Opus Dei campaign to have Monsignor Escrivá declared a saint has been thorough. Even though the founder died as recently as 1975, changes made in 1985 in the procedure for canonisation allow for the canonisation of a person once they are ten years deceased.

Chapter 4

Personal Testament

This chapter deals with some personal experiences of Irish people and others who have come into contact with Opus Dei in a variety of ways. It is based mainly on the response to a notice placed in the Irish national press in February 1987 requesting comments and experiences from readers with regard to the movement. In the newspaper notices it was stated that replies would be treated confidentially. This was vital as it subsequently transpired that many people were afraid of publicly speaking out against the movement or being individually identified as ex-Opus Dei members. Others were afraid of recriminations or of being victimised.

* * *

One of the most famous defectors from Opus Dei was Dr John Roche, who teaches the history of science at Linacre College, Oxford, England. Dr Roche took Opus Dei to court in London in 1981 for the return of £20,000 which he claimed had been taken from him during his fourteen years with the organisation. He joined Opus Dei in 1959 as a 22 - year-old graduate student at University College Galway, when he was studying for a Master's degree in electromagnetism. Dr Roche became a numerary member and a Director of Opus Dei in Ireland. He also met the founder, Monsignor Escrivá, on a number of occasions in Spain. Dr Roche:

> I was deeply religious, friendly and extrovert, busily involved in Catholic action, a teetotaller, desperately shy with women, successful in my academic studies, and living at home in a warm family situation. Early in 1959 a colleague recommended me to a Lenten retreat in the Gort Ard University Residence which had recently been opened by Opus Dei in Galway. I had never heard of Opus Dei until then but my friend assured me that they were dynamic Catholic professionals and university people. I went along to the retreat during which I had personal spiritual guidance from the visiting Spanish priest who gave it, and the head of Opus Dei in Ireland, and afterwards I had a delightful get-together with the members of Opus Dei who were all laymen, except for that priest.
>
> I was immediately impressed by Opus Dei. They invested religious practice with a vitality and elegance which was totally new to me. The members displayed an enthusiasm, a seriousness of purpose, a confidence, and a radiant idealism which was quite overpowering. I was also made the centre of an admiring and affectionate group and became particularly friendly with a young lawyer, Tom, who was also a well-known rugby player, and who arranged to meet me after the retreat. After several months, I joined Opus Dei, quite voluntarily.
>
> Shortly after I joined I went to live in Gort Ard, only a few miles away from my home. My parents were very unhappy about this since I was the eldest, but they did not oppose me. Life in that house was an extraordinary experience. According

to the jargon of Opus Dei, as soon as I moved in my "honeymoon" was over. I was immediately caught up in hectic activity and in relationships with other members, which provoked in me intense feelings alternating between exhilaration, exhaustion and oppressiveness. This activity, apart from my professional work, consisted in strenuous efforts to complete every day the large number of religious practices; attending the frequent classes of formation; meditations, get-togethers, and private chats with the priest and lay director, which were intended to ensure a rapid formation of new members. Doing duties about the house, making attempts to contact people with money and, most important of all, I was pressed to recruit intensely among my student friends, day and night. Opus Dei will always be a reminder to me how much activity can be packed into one day.

There was a certain madcap side to recruitment and indeed to personal relations among the younger members. I was encouraged to use occasional foul language in my apostolate since it was regarded as more secular and manly and attracted the young potential recruits. Members of Opus Dei were encouraged to do occasional "crazy" things in their apostolate. For example, while I was being recruited a member drove me home at an alarming speed up a steep hill, while I sat on my bicycle desperately hanging on to the window of his car. Opus Dei was full of stories of doings of this sort and we boasted with some truth, perhaps, how superior this was to the sickly piosity of some religious orders. "Holy Joes" were scorned.

For the first three months or so a spark of critical judgement survived in me. I noticed occasional outbursts of ill temper among members and resolved to try to improve the atmosphere in the house. On one occasion I challenged a priest for having stated in a meditation that members must learn to "identify their personalities with the personality of their director." We were frequently told, however, that a critical spirit about Opus Dei was contrary to the will of God. My ability to take a detached, critical, view of Opus Dei soon disappeared.

Opus Dei gradually filled my whole world, everything else being pushed to the margin. It was a world very much apart from civil society and from the rest of the Church. It was self-centered and exhilarated by its own sense of destiny. The priests listened to the Top Twenty so that they could chat to the younger members or possible recruits at their level. The house at Gort Ard was spotlessly clean, comfortable, and the furnishings improved steadily with the prosperity of the region. The members looked up directly at the Host during the elevation of the Blessed Sacrament and did not cower before God as others did. The Rosary was said slowly in disciplined unison; Holy Mass was celebrated with exquisite dignity and reverence, genuflections were done properly. Members dressed expensively but with sober taste, thought of themselves as part of the higher echelons of the secular society, and were frequently encouraged to have a superiority complex. This many certainly did have, particularly with respect to Catholic action and to the clergy "not of the Work."

I was soon introduced to further "family customs" such as having my incoming and outgoing letters read, handing over my salary, sleeping on the floor once a week (another mortification for the Father) and the weekly *discipline* which consisted in private self-flagellation of forty lashes with a waxed corded whip. We were encouraged to "draw a little blood" and frequently told how the "Father" drew so much blood that he spattered the walls and ceiling with it. I loathed the discipline. It made my flesh creep to overhear others taking it. I went to sleep depressed at the prospect of taking it the following morning. My conscience gnawed at me to take it more frequently and I approached my director hoping he would not give me the go-ahead. For the next thirteen years I took the discipline three times a week. It was a constant source of depression although in my final years it affected me less. I discovered later that a director is supposed to take the discipline more frequently still, and more violently, when someone in his care is having problems of vocation. As the years passed I grew more strained and withdrawn. Vast areas of personal growth were stunted by these and other practices.

About half of the numeraries in the house had personality disorders, of varying degrees of severity, and the Spanish priest in charge was quite pathological. He would occasionally break into a rage at some provocation or other and treat the object of his wrath with the most scalding abuse. My anxieties grew and grew. I constantly felt guilty about my failure to recruit a lot of new members, my failure to find rich people who would give money to Opus Dei, my failure to complete the "norms" down to the last detail and about my failure to do sufficient mortification. I began to dread get-togethers with the Spanish priest because of his tense and forced merriment, his oppressiveness, his moods and his presumption of absolute control over our lives. When he occasionally went to Dublin for a few days, what a relief! When I was made a director in 1965 I tried to articulate my unspoken feelings and to apply them in my guidance of the younger numeraries and new recruits. Of course I preserved intact the structures and practices of Opus Dei, but I worked out new apostolic concepts, new notions of freedom, obedience, mortification and virtue, and above all I elaborated in great detail the concept of work. The importance of ordinary work as a means of salvation was Opus Dei's great new message to the Catholic Church.

One day as I lay in bed with a cold, it suddenly flashed upon me that this was the only Catholic association I knew of which talked incessantly about "spreading the spirit of Opus Dei" rather than spreading the spirit of Jesus Christ.

Over a period of time I began to write down my criticisms and hand them over to my director, which is exactly how Opus Dei allows members to criticise, except that one is recommended to tear up the criticism once it is written down.

We were visited from time to time by the Procurator General of Opus Dei—the third in its hierarchy. This man had an air of absolute authority. On one occasion he sent the Regional Counsellor rushing along the corridor to tell me to stop singing. On another occasion I witnessed the whole Regional Commission racing up in alarm from the playing fields because the Procurator had a girl on our tennis court and wanted me, the Warden, to make sure she did not use the changing room. After one of his visits all of the locks were removed from bedroom doors and from students' wardrobes because of the possibility of clandestine liaisons with women. The number of beds in each room was made an odd number to reduce the risk of homosexuality. Pornographic books were removed and sometimes burned, provoking considerable anger among the students.

As the years moved on more and more anxieties crowded into my life, as a result of the incoherent demands of Opus Dei. I felt a growing tension between the secular image of an ordinary Christian layman, which we were supposed to constantly project among our colleagues, and the reality of my narrow celibate life with its vows of poverty, chastity and obedience and its hostility to intellectual culture. We were told to deny that we had vows, and to conceal our membership of Opus Dei. Reading was heavily censored. No holidays were allowed. We were not allowed to give presents, even at family occasions such as weddings, and if invited to the theatre we were instructed to say that we did not feel like it. We were taught never to make Opus Dei responsible for anything unpleasant, when indeed it was often utterly responsible.

After thirteen years in Opus Dei I still had not warmed to it. It was the cross God had asked me to bear and I did not expect to like it. When the opportunity to visit Spain and meet the Father arose I had great expectations. I hoped to find a reason to like Opus Dei. I hoped to discover some personal quality in the Father which I could like and which would explain to me the delirious admiration for him in Opus Dei.

In the event I took away very mixed feelings from Spain. But it was an unforgettable experience. On the one hand there was the intense activity, the great ambition, the flood of recruits, the glittering buildings, the sheer vibrating energy of the whole enterprise, and many likeable people. On the negative side there was everything I had already disliked in Opus Dei, only here it was pushed to utterly harsh extremes. The hatred by Opus Dei members of the local clergy was almost frenzied. On one occasion I was chatting to an Irish priest of Opus Dei in the university grounds when he suddenly drew me aside, pointed to a Franciscan walking along the path and said, in English, "let's get out of the way, dirt is coming."

All of the university residences in the city, not run by Opus Dei were endlessly castigated. Many of the older members were visibly distressed.

I had met the Father, Monsignor Escrivá, on several occasions over the years in Ireland and in Rome, but now I was 36, I had recovered my sense of personal identity and the ability to think for myself, and was determined not to be overwhelmed by the general adulation.

We were arranged in circles around a settee where the Father was going to sit, about fifty of us, all numeraries. When he came in everyone sprang to their feet. He was accompanied by Fr Alvaro del Portillo, the present President General.

Monsignor Escrivá had an expression on his face which is indelibly printed on my memory. It was a look of rage mingled with horror. I was astounded by this and asked the numerary beside me what was going on. He just laughed it off. Monsignor Escrivá quickly composed himself and sat on the settee inviting me and another Kenyan numerary to sit beside him. I smiled warmly at Fr Alvaro del Portillo but he viewed me with utter coldness throughout the get-together. What I saw beside me was Escrivá, a small priest of about seventy, burning with a feverish energy, not very refined, vain, moody, restless, with impersonal eyes, incapable or unwilling to communicate with me as an individual, but thriving on collective banter as the centre of a gathering which worshipped him totally and feared him to the point of terror. When he gestured to us to sit down, most sat on the floor and everyone took out their diaries, where they had written questions to ask the Father, and wrote down his replies. Indeed this get-together was tape-recorded and many others were filmed. I wrote down a great deal and I was much in demand subsequently to talk about the Father.

I told everyone afterwards that I felt no infatuation and they could not understand it. Undoubtedly the Father had charisma but it was not granted to me to perceive it. On another occasion, in an effort to awaken in myself a feeling of affection for him, I jumped up and gave him a bear hug. It seemed to startle him. One of the numeraries accompanying him whispered to me that the Father had quite liked my gesture, and hinted that it would do me good. This was my first inkling of internal politics within Opus Dei.

Early in the summer of 1973 I assembled all of my notes and began to write up a very carefully documented report on what I considered to be the abuses in Opus Dei. Although, theoretically, this is how one is supposed to present criticism in Opus Dei, my directors were not at all happy about it, especially when I told them that I was also keeping a diary. Events began to move very quickly. I was asked to hand over immediately what I had written, but refused. About a week later I had a very unpleasant meeting with a Spanish member of the General Council of Opus Dei. Realising that time was running out, I secretly Xeroxed a large selection of what I considered to be the most revealing internal documents, because I knew that without such evidence I could do nothing about Opus Dei.

Shortly afterwards I was called to the English headquarters of Opus Dei in London and formally interrogated. A typewritten list of my questions was read to me and my answers noted down. I was then solemnly admonished by the Counsellor, asked to retract my criticisms, and asked to hand over my half-written report. I refused to comply. I asked whether the Father was infallible and I was informed that it was more likely that he was infallible than I. I was then told that I would not be allowed to live in a house of Opus Dei for the present, because I might harm the younger numeraries.

Penniless, I went to live with my parents in Galway, and continued writing up my report. I had frequent meetings with the Irish counsellor of Opus Dei whom I liked. When he heard my criticisms (that Opus Dei was totalitarian; that the Father was a tyrant over consciences; that Opus Dei was presenting a completely false picture of itself to the world) not unnaturally he became angry and forbade me to speak of my views to any member in Ireland, except another designated priest. This I accepted.

After some time I was called to Gort Ard in Galway to talk to the Procurator General of Opus Dei. He was very civilised and much easier to deal with than anyone else I had encountered in the higher levels of Opus Dei. Nevertheless he was very firm indeed. He told me that as a condition of membership I had to believe that the Father was divinely inspired, and that in matters of the spirit of

Opus Dei he could not err. I asked to see the
Constitution of Opus Dei to discover my rights but
was refused. I asked to speak to a canon lawyer in
the Work but again I was refused. My presumption
in attempting to reform Opus Dei was regarded as
nothing less than an outrage against the Work. I
was informed that if I did not retract my criticisms
and hand over immediately what I had written, I
would be expelled from Opus Dei. I was given until
the following afternoon to comply.

I Xeroxed my report, and handed over the
original the following afternoon, but refused to
retract my criticisms and warned that if I was
expelled I would immediately take up the matter
with the Vatican. I still saw my future in Opus Dei,
but as a reformer, and I wanted the Father to read
my report at least before I was expelled. I sent
express letters to the Father and to Fr Alvaro del
Portillo complaining of the complete refusal to
consider my evidence seriously and of the
infallibility claimed for the Father. I soon became
aware that there was already telephone
communication with Rome over the affair.

I was not expelled. I got my scholarship at
Oxford University and returned there in October.
In November the Counsellor of Opus Dei in
Ireland, following a trip to Rome which included
my case, came to see me in Oxford. He told me that
the Father rejected my report. It was admitted that
"I knew a lot about Opus Dei" but I had caused a
great deal of trouble and would never again be
allowed in a house of Opus Dei. After this I decided
to resign and did so in November 1973. I was
released from my vows.

* * *

Kevin Mahon (not his real name) works as a doctor in one of Dublin's leading hospitals. He has been an outspoken opponent of Opus Dei and its methods of recruitment for many years:

> Early in 1982 I was visited at the hospital at which I was working by a priest who claimed to be a member of Opus Dei. He stated that he knew that I was responsible for an article which appeared about Opus Dei in one of the Sunday newspapers, and also for literature of an adverse nature about Opus Dei which was posted to a number of hospital doctors' staff rooms. He stated that if I ceased criticising Opus Dei all would be forgiven but that if I should ever criticise them again my employers would be informed, I would be sacked and become unemployable. He also claimed that most senior members of the medical professional were members of Opus Dei. I know now that this is incorrect. However, I was aware that Opus Dei was making a major attempt to recruit medical students, mainly from U.C.G., and having previously worked in the West of Ireland I knew some students whom I considered to be at special risk. I also had the full backing of one set of parents and the family of another member who were rather bewildered that their daughter could be so alienated from them by what they perceived to be a Catholic institution. I therefore posted out what I considered to be factual material about Opus Dei which I had just obtained from Dr John Roche and a psychologist in Liverpool whose daughter had been recruited into the organisation.
>
> A few days after posting, I received a telephone call from the same Opus Dei priest who demanded to see me. The phone call was unpleasant and

contained veiled threats of an unspecified nature. I
arranged to see him that afternoon at the hospital.
However, as I was somewhat worried about what
the meeting would entail, I contacted a senior
public official whose daughter had been recruited
without his knowledge or consent. He advised me
to record the conversation with a concealed tape
recorder and that if I were threatened or assaulted,
to involve the police. I also attempted to contact my
union, the Irish Medical Organisation, for advice
but was unable to do so.

As soon as my "guest" arrived he appeared to be
both aggressive and agitated. I conducted him into
the room that I had set aside for the purpose and
the conversation got underway. My visitor stated
that he had not come to debate or discuss the issue
but had come to warn me of the consequences of
my action. My career was definitely finished. The
entire medical establishment had been informed of
my actions. I was unemployable and Opus Dei
were exploring ways of removing my name from
the medical register. As a result I would never be
able to practise anywhere in the world.
Furthermore, my family would be informed and
disgraced. I was on the point of being sued and
would spend my life paying off heavy legal bills.
My health would suffer —he did not specify how.
He said my action was pointless as nothing could
hurt Opus Dei or stop the organisation. However,
at this stage my tape recorder made a rather loud
click as one side had ended. My visitor became very
angry. He threw the table aside in which the
recorder was concealed and tried to pull out the
cassette. I attempted to prevent him and a full scale
tussle ensued which lasted a couple of minutes.
Unfortunately he succeeded in depriving me of the

tape and ripped it from the cassette. When he discovered matches on a nearby table he tried to burn the tape, but only parts of it melted. Eventually he tore it into smaller sections and threw it into a wastepaper basked. When my "guest" departed he informed me that there was no hope for me in this life or the next and that I had in fact excommunicated myself from the Church. When he was gone I recovered the tape and with the help of friends attempted to restore it. This was only partially successful.

In the years that followed I received a number of hostile and anonymous telephone calls concerning my criticisms of Opus Dei. My parents also received a number of calls. I have no idea who could be responsible for these except they all referred to Opus Dei and doubted if I could ever be saved. The calls became more frequent around the time of the *Magill* magazine investigation into Opus Dei published in May 1983. Some time afterwards I was visited by Opus Dei again.

By this time I had changed jobs to another hospital and was busy in the casualty department when my next "patient" happened to be a supernumerary member of Opus Dei. I had known this individual for some months previously. He used to hang around University College Dublin chatting to other students about the nearby Cleraun University Residence, which had recently opened. I was somewhat surprised at seeing him but he quickly put me in the picture. He advised me to step outside of the casualty department as there would be less of a fuss. Despite a number of patients waiting I complied, as I did not wish to draw attention to myself from the other staff.

Once outside I was met by another priest of

Opus Dei who this time was quite friendly. He listened to my objections to Opus Dei and denied in a friendly way that I had any grounds for complaint. He assured me that Opus Dei had vast influence in Ireland and said my opposition to them would only damage myself and that Opus Dei was considering legal action. He departed with the supernumerary wishing me well but telling me I had lots of grounds for worry.

Sometime after that incident I was visited by the same priest who suggested that I should read the newspapers in the coming weeks as Opus Dei were about to be honoured. I did so, and in the following weeks Opus Dei was appointed as a Personal Prelature to the Roman Catholic Church—a position they had always sought. I felt that one of the more popular Irish morning newspapers was over-enthusiastic about Opus Dei's achievements and so submitted some of the material in my possession to the newspaper's religious affairs correspondent. I did not meet him but submitted the material with my name and address, asking for confidentiality. It was arranged that I would meet the correspondent at noon the following day. However, early the next morning, the same Opus Dei priest visited me and told me not to be foolish by seeing this newspaper correspondent. The correspondent, according to the priest, had rung him the previous evening to ask who I was and to explain that nothing critical of Opus Dei would be published. I was very disappointed that my confidentiality had not been honoured and rang the newspaper editor to complain. He apologised and assured me that he would look into the incident. He said he was unaware that his religious affairs correspondent was a member of Opus Dei.

Since then I have received no other visits from Opus Dei people. The telephone calls have ceased.

* * *

Dermot Roantree is a present-day member of Opus Dei, studying for a Doctorate in History at University College Dublin. He lives in the Nullamore University Residence Centre in Dartry and offered the following testimony :

One of the misfortunes of the media attention that has been paid to Opus Dei over the last while is that basic and rather ordinary facts have been more and more obscured by an unceasing search for the extraordinary. The truth, unfortunately, can often be boring. It generally has a hard time getting around and getting itself heard. Myths, on the other hand, have wings. And they have a most captivating way of expressing themselves.

In 1986, a full hour's programme about Opus Dei on the air-waves could still produce a question from a caller which ran like this : "Do these people go to Mass and confession like Catholics do?" the presenter responded, in a suitably exasperated tone, "Caller, they *are* Catholics!" and went on to say something to the effect that when talking of Opus Dei one is talking of a more intensely lived Catholic life. A good answer, but I may be excused for having serious doubts about the value of any kind of media coverage which could provoke that question in the first place.

And so, even in a personal testimony such as this, I find it necessary to outline some basic facts about Opus Dei. After all, nothing that I say about myself and Opus Dei can be properly understood without these facts being kept firmly in mind. For the Opus

Dei I joined is not the Opus Dei that is frequently sensationalised in certain media. It is, instead, an Opus Dei that is Catholic in its very essence. It is an Opus Dei that has the full approval of the Church; that has the blessings of the last five Popes; that is loyal to the teachings of the Church; that has an exclusively supernatural and apostolic aim; and that bases its whole mission on a profound sense of Christian freedom.

If someone were to ask me what my religion is, I would of course tell him that I am a Catholic. If he were not very familiar with Catholic doctrine and wished to know more, I would hand him some slim volume which outlines the Church's beliefs. He might, however, press me further. He might say to me : "This is all very well. But how do Catholics act on it? And how do *you* act on it ?"

It is only at this point that I would have cause to mention Opus Dei. I would explain to my inquirer that there are many ways of imitating Christ in the Catholic Church, and that one of the signs of the Church's vitality is that every so often in her history a fresh insight has led to the formation of a new spirituality—a new way of looking for God and finding Him in this world. One of these I would continue, is Opus Dei.

For over thirty years before the Second Vatican Council gave its central message to the world—that everyone (not only priests and religious) is called by Christ to try to be a saint—this message was embodied in the lay spirituality of Opus Dei. And recently, by erecting Opus Dei as a Personal Prelature, the Church has entrusted it with a specific pastoral mission. That is, to remind people of the universal call to holiness and to provide, in the spirit peculiar to Opus Dei, a help towards attaining that holiness. Members of Opus Dei are ordinary lay people, married, single or widowed. They do not take vows. Rather, they commit themselves to practise all the Christian virtues in the course of their everyday work and in their social and domestic duties. "That," I would say to my inquirer in conclusion, "is the way that God wants *me* to act on those beliefs you have been reading. Others He has called to other ways; me, He has called to Opus Dei."

My first contact with Opus Dei was as a member of Nullamore Junior Club in Dublin. In the footsteps of my older brothers I attended the club each week. Apart from the normal activities of a youth club, we had a weekly talk from the chaplain, usually on some virtue—faith, hope, love, cheerfulness, loyalty to one's friends, obedience to one's parents and so on. For a number of years I was one of a group of six or seven relatives and friends who went to the club. But at the age of fourteen or fifteen new circumstances—including some changes in schools, in friendships, and in attitudes—led to my companions deciding, more or less as a group, to divert their social energies elsewhere and to cease having regular contact with a centre of Opus Dei. They continued, however, to have (and still have) fond memories of the craft activities, the debating, the sports, hikes, and camps, and to have more or less positive appreciation of the religious formation they had received. I was the only one of the group who decided to continue receiving that formation. I could easily have opted out with my friends. But I did not want to.

In the course of the next few years I thought more and more about the possibility of joining Opus Dei. When eventually I talked to the director of the centre about it I was told clearly that what was in question was a divine vocation and I was urged to think and pray more about it. I did so, and I was asked a lot of questions before I asked to join. Before I was admitted, however, I had a long talk with my parents. They understood well, and were very pleased and supportive. The only concern my father expressed on that occasion was that if anything happened to him (he was not in good health and knew that he had not that long to live) I would be able to help my mother in whatever way necessary. I was able to assure him that I would do so, just like any other member of my family. I was admitted to Opus Dei shortly afterwards.

There you have it—the rather banal history of one vocation. Banal, that is, for everyone except me. The progress of every human life is dramatic, but usually only for the person himself. I am quite sure that my brothers and sisters, most of whom have followed their own vocations in recent years, would agree with me on this. Four of them are now married, some with families; and two of my sisters have entered the religious life. Each of us has made a conscientious decision and said "Yes" to his or her own thing. We might equally have said "No." That is the drama of it; and the drama continues throughout our lives, for to make a success of a vocation one has to reaffirm one's original commitment each day. A vocation to Opus Dei is no exception in this regard. I joined freely and I stay freely.

I might add here that because of changed circumstances some of the people in my family are unable to be around the family home very often. Yet we continue to be very close indeed. Doubtless this is because we each understand and respect the commitments of the others. But these qualities of understanding and respect are sadly lacking in those who observe Opus Dei on the lookout for what is newsworthy or sensational and who don't mind prying into the most intimate aspects of life in Opus Dei for the sake of satisfying a morbid curiosity. And I don't think it is too hard to say that to do this in public amounts to a practical violence against personal consciences.

It is patently irreverent and impertinent to ask someone about the intimacies of his or her marital relations; I would like to think it is equally clear that the particulars of how I decided freely to follow Christ in Opus Dei are my own business. How I pray, how often I pray, how I mortify myself, how often I mortify myself, what means I use to realise the presence of God while I work and while I relax, how I use my time: these are all essentially personal matters and they ought not to be up for public scrutiny and anyone with a modicum of moral sensitivity can see that I say this not because my relationship with God is secret but because it is private. There is a radical difference.

That point made clear, however, I feel I must say something more explicit about the ascetical life of those in Opus Dei. But I do so only because I am afraid people will misconstrue my silence if I don't. I have this much to say: some members—and only some—use some means of corporal mortification, means which have a venerable place in the history of the Church. To say that they lost this mark of venerability with the Second Vatican Council is to misinterpret or misrepresent badly the ascetical theology of that council. Indeed, members of Opus Dei are not the only ones in the Church who use these means, and those members who do use them use them in a relatively moderate way. They do not form a basis of a spirit of self-denial. Far more important and far more spectacular (in the eyes of God if not in the eyes of journalists) is the minute-to-minute fight to smile when one doesn't feel like smiling, to work when one doesn't feel like working, to think about others when one prefers to think about oneself. These little struggles are much more illustrative of the essence of Opus Dei's spirituality than the moderate use of corporal mortification; and, unlike the latter, they mark the lives of all members of Opus Dei. Anyone who would like to know more about the details of this spirituality and about the theology which informs it can consult the writings of the founder of Opus Dei, Monsignor Escrivá; or, indeed, one could talk to a member of Opus Dei.

In fact, it has often happened that someone has had many false notions about Opus Dei dispelled simply by talking them over with a member. It is all too easy for a perverted view of Opus Dei to take firm root in a person's mind when there is no contact with the members themselves, and all that is known is learned from dubious sources.

I remember, somewhat in this context, one evening some years ago when I was talking to another postgraduate in the college where I was studying, whom I had just met for the first time. While we talked a lecturer from our department popped his head in and out of the door. When he had gone, my new acquaintance turned to me and, cupping one hand around his mouth, whispered, "Be careful with him. He's in Opus Dei." "No, no." I responded immediately. "You have it all wrong. *He* is not in Opus Dei; but *I* am." When the colour returned to his face he stammered something about secrecy, but as I had just been rather forthright about my own membership the charge seemed to lose much of its force. I think I did explain to him, however, that my commitments to Opus Dei are personal and not public. I represent only myself. I am an ordinary citizen and an ordinary layman. My opinions—professional, political, cultural and so on—are my own and not Opus Dei's. Yet anyone who knows me knows that I am in Opus Dei and I have no interest in keeping it a secret. I most certainly would never deny it. A few minutes after our conversation, in fact, my colleague learned that my membership of Opus Dei was common knowledge among those lecturers who knew me. Indeed, if members of Opus Dei are secretive, they have a lot to learn about how to keep a secret.

He also tackled me, however, on the charge that Opus Dei is elitist—that is, it's only interested in catering for the rich middle-classes and only want members with university degrees. I told him a little about the Anchor Club in Artane, the largest club in Ireland in which Opus Dei is involved, which caters mainly for apprentices and young workers. "But why don't you publicise these things?", my companion retorted. He had a point. But then again, it is not as easy as it seems. "If somebody falls out a club-house window or if the premises go up in smoke, you'll probably hear about it," I replied. He understood what I meant.

One thing which people very often do not understand, however, is that Opus Dei's relationship with its members extends only as far as their spiritual lives. It has not the slightest interest in telling a member how to do his or her job, beyond saying that it should be done well and conscientiously. It has no interest in telling me what opinions to hold or what conclusions to reach in my historical research. Nor is it interested in telling me what politics to hold.

As regards my politics, I would simply quote the philosopher Jacques Maritain, and say that I stand with him. He says, after expressing considerable disdain for both 'left' and 'right', that "I feel myself less distant from the first when it is a question of things that are Caesar's and less distant from the second (alas!) when it is a question of the things that are God's." Other people in Opus Dei might find this a wholly unsatisfactory position to adopt. That is their privilege. I don't ask them to agree with me. In fact, I have very little idea of the politics of most of the people in Opus Dei that I know.

Membership of Opus Dei is a divine vocation. Very many people have received a lifetime of spiritual and doctrinal formation from Opus Dei without ever becoming members. Indeed, Monsignor Escrivá's own sister dedicated her entire life to helping her brother, mainly by organising the domestic administration of many of the first centres of Opus Dei in Spain and Italy. Yet she never joined Opus Dei. She simply did not have a vocation. And many people found their vocation to religious orders thanks to the spiritual guidance of Monsignor Escrivá. He saw that it was to *that* that God was calling them and not to Opus Dei.

For him the notion that every person has to find God according to the call of his or her own conscience, and in full freedom, was a matter of critical pastoral importance. He was immensely fond of the anarchist slogan which he saw scrawled on a wall during the Spanish Civil War : "Let each wayfarer make his own way." He insisted on such pluralism when it came to anyone setting out to choose a way in life. And he insisted on absolute freedom when it came to anyone making a definitive choice. "Wanting to" is an equally essential condition of remaining there. I would like to think that everyone—and especially those who have some responsibility for the shaping of public opinion — could share such refinement and respect in thinking or talking about the conscientious choice of a way of life of every individual. That way all Christians — indeed, all men—could live in the fullness of what St Paul called the "freedom of the children of God."

* * *

Mark Kelly (not his real name) joined Opus Dei Gort Ard university residence for men in Salthill, Galway some years back. The experiences of that time remain vivid in his memory.

The daily rhythm of religious practices and "family customs" was somewhat as follows. At Gort Ard we were awakened at seven in the morning and encouraged to practise the "heroic minute," that is to jump out of the bed immediately and kiss the floor saying "serviam", I serve. This was followed by a second piece of heroism, a cold shower which I dreaded at first but soon learned to tolerate. It was a mortification for 'the Father'. We had exactly half an hour to wash and dress, in complete silence, and punctual attendance in the oratory at half-seven was a matter of considerable importance.

Indeed, there was an air of competition about who could get there first. A half-hour of meditation followed, which normally involved reflection on a group of points from *The Way*. Sometimes this meditation was given by a priest and this was felt to be less strenuous mentally than private meditation.

After the meditation there was Holy Mass and Communion followed by ten minutes of thanksgiving. The Director started and terminated each of these common acts with a special prayer. Breakfast was an informal meal but at other meals the director sat at the head of the table with the priest of the local council at his right hand and was provided with a small bell for calling the domestic staff. When lunch was completed we would visit the Blessed Sacrament and have a half-hour to get together. During the afternoon there was a minor silence while one wore the *cilis*. It was especially worn around the upper thigh so that the marks would not be visible when playing sports. The full fifteen mysteries of the Rosary were recited each day. One part was said in common but one had to find gaps in the day for other parts. It was a constant anxiety to get the whole Rosary completed before bedtime. If one failed to do so, as indeed with any of the other duties, one mentioned to the spiritual director and he at his discretion could waive it or ask you to do it before going to bed. In later years this obligation was reduced to five mysteries of the Rosary and a brief meditation on the remaining mysteries.

There was a half-hour private meditation in the evenings. This was the best moment of the day for me. It provided the freedom to be alone with a compassionate God who transcended even the authority of Opus Dei. There was a half-hour get-together of the members before retiring for the night. This was intended to be a joyous occasion and it often was. Jokes and laughter were not uncommon. We often discussed with great excitement the new recruits about to join our house. Regularly reminding each other of the sheer wonder of Opus Dei, of how blessed and privileged we were to be members; of many brilliant and famous people there were in the work and of the astounding plans God had in store for the movement. We pitied and ridiculed the lazy, dirty and reprobate religious orders and secular clergy. I was frequently overcome by transports of euphoria.

After these get-togethers there was a brief commentary on the Gospel, we kissed the floor and said a prayer for Opus Dei, the Father, the Pope and the local Bishop. This was followed by an examination of conscience. A major silence then began which was not interrupted until breakfast the next morning. Before getting into bed one sprinkled it with Holy Water and said three Hail Marys with arms outstretched for holy purity.

Mark has since left Opus Dei and now works in England.

* * *

In 1981 the Connollys (not their real name) sent their daughter Mary (not her real name) to study medicine at University College Galway. Instead of living in a flat it was decided that a suitable university residence would be much nicer and so Mary moved into the Ros Geal centre for women on University Road. Neither she nor her parents were aware that it was run by Opus Dei members. At this early stage they had never heard of the organisation.

All was going well until the first summer holiday period arrived. Mrs Connolly takes up the story :

Mary rang and told us she was not coming home

and gave us all sorts of excuses. When we eventually persuaded her to come home for the holidays she was inundated with daily telephone calls from Opus Dei members in Galway asking her to return. We only discovered at a later stage that money, gifts, everything we were sending her was being handed over to Opus Dei in Galway. As parents we were very much left on the outside while our daughter was slowly being recruited into the movement. During the holidays Mary was given work as a courier for some Spanish students by Opus Dei in return for which she was to receive one hundred pounds. When the work was finished she was refused the money but offered a course in lieu at the Ballyglunin Conference Centre, Tuam, run by Opus Dei members. We began to see less and less of her. She told us that she had a new family in Opus Dei. There was a marked change in her personality. Whenever she did visit home, she appeared distant and somehow different. On some occasions she would make notes of her conservations with us in a diary which was later discussed with her spiritual director at Ros Geal. It was not until the eve of her examinations that we discovered she had joined Opus Dei during her first year at the residence centre.

Mary was under eighteen years of age when she was recruited into Opus Dei. She was twenty-one when her mother was told. On one occasion when her parents travelled to Galway to take her home for summer holidays and a surprise trip to the Holy Land, they discovered she had been transferred at the last moment to Carrickburn Study Centre in Donnybrook, Dublin. All efforts to persuade Mary to leave Opus Dei were strongly resisted. She told her parents "not to be doing the work of the Devil".

In 1986 Mrs Connolly was contacted by researchers on the RTE *Live Line* Radio Show in connection with a proposed programme on Opus Dei. She decided to be interviewed for the broadcast. After the RTE researchers had contacted Opus Dei for their comments on Mrs Connolly's case an Opus Dei official made desperate attempts to contact Mary to have her counter the allegations. It was to be a mother versus daughter showdown. A few hours before the broadcast Mary contacted her mother and they made an arrangement to meet in the Burlington Hotel in Dublin. She told her mother that if she went ahead with the interview she would never speak to her again, never visit home or contact her parents. Mary insisted that her mother cancel the proposed interview. The Connollys are convinced that their daughter was used by Opus Dei to try and dissuade the family from speaking out against the movement. In the end, Mrs Connolly went ahead with her interview. Opus Dei declined to be interviewed for the programme. However Mary rang the live radio show and on the air denounced her mother's allegations.

Today Mary is lecturing in medicine at University College Dublin. She is a numerary member of Opus Dei and visits her parents six times a year. She insists that Opus Dei has given her life a new meaning and real happiness. Her welfare is a source of constant concern to her parents who can only see her, aside from rare home visits, at Carrickburn and then by arrangement only.

* * *

Mrs Williams (not her real name) saw an advertisement for a catering course in her local newspaper. A friend recommended it. She visited Crannton Catering and Educational Centre in Dartry, Dublin and was very impressed. She was unaware that the establishment was run by Opus Dei members. Her daughter was enrolled in July but Mrs Williams had decided to withdraw her by the following November. As a parent she was concerned about the difficulty in getting her daughter released to visit home on weekends. On one occasion, considerable pressure had to be applied to the staff of the centre before they were willing to allow Mrs Williams's daughter home for a family funeral. When she did come home, life in the catering college revealed some surprises.

Mrs. Williams explains what happened:

> Sarah told us when she came home that letters my husband and I had sent her were opened and read by the teachers in the college. I had also sent my daughter a parcel on her birthday but it had not been given to her. Instead the staff at Crannton opened it and divided the contents around all the girls. I was very upset when Sarah told me this. Later she explained how the members of Opus Dei at the college had a "new family." She would not be able to come home for Christmas because Christmas was always spent with "the family." During her time at Crannton pressure was put on Sarah to join Opus Dei and to visit Rome on a proposed trip the following Easter. At the time she knew herself that it was not the right time to make such a big decision. Because she was the only one in her class not to have joined the organisation, Sarah decided to leave before she was eventually persuaded otherwise. At seventeen, she was not ready to make such a major commitment. I felt my

parental influence over my daughter was being deliberately diminished by the staff at Crannton. Whenever I called to Dublin to visit her the other Opus Dei members were always in and out of the room so a private conversation was impossible. It was as though she was being watched all the time. There was no privacy.

Life was carefully controlled for the girls at Crannton. Radios were not allowed; watching television was rationed and the programmes chosen for them. The girls were not allowed to make telephone calls. They had no money. The day was filled from early morning to bedtime with domestic works, study or religious devotions. Many of the girls trained and worked in the nearby Opus Dei Nullamore University Residence Centre for men but were forbidden to speak to any of the male students. Mrs Williams resented the strictness of the lifestyle. Her daughter only met Opus Dei members. Contact with the outside world was impossible. Even contact with her family was restricted. Mrs Williams spoke to Sarah and it was eventually decided that she should leave. After one more visit home, her family decided to collect Sarah's belongings.

Mrs Williams :

We left her sitting in our car with a few friends. I had to go in and tell the director of the college that my daughter was leaving. When I asked for her case and clothes they refused to give them. Eventually we found Sarah's case and had to carry out her clothes. As we were leaving one of the teachers came out and when she saw Sarah in the car remarked "I know why you are leaving and you know why you are leaving but we won't tell your mother" as if our daughter had committed some crime. It was like blackmail. I know my daughter has nothing to be ashamed of.

* * *

Dr Denys Turner teaches theology in Bristol University, England. In 1960 he was studying at University College Dublin and living in the Opus Dei Nullamore University Residence Centre. He became a numerary member and later Director of the Ely Study Centre and Residence at Hume Street.

Dr. Turner :

The pressure to recruit new members was very much a matter of bad conscience as far as I was concerned. Recruitment was something which was regarded almost as a test of how well a person was living out their vocation in Opus Dei. The "by your fruits you will know them" kind of talk was common. Recruitment became almost bureaucratised so that targets were set for each individual. The paradox of this is that since Opus Dei teaches the idea that recruitment is possible only through friendships with people, the combination of the notion of friendship with the bureaucratisation of pressure made friendship a very artificial, a very forced thing. One of the areas I found difficult to adjust to after leaving the movement was having a perfectly ordinary relationship with someone. I wanted to have relationships with people because I enjoyed them rather than having an interest in taking somebody by means of friendship to a particular goal I had rather than one which they had. It was an exploitation of friendship which should always be something natural. This set up tensions and contradictions within my personality and in others I met.

On criticism of the movement Dr Turner points out :

Opus Dei tends to regard criticism as a threat and the organisation becomes exceptionally defensive. Members are commonly quite incapable of seeing themselves as other people see them. They do not appear to understand their place within the overall context of a varied church. When you are in the organisation you simply cannot see anything from the point of view of those outside it. In that sense it does produce a very introverted, inward looking, self-conscious movement. Opus Dei is, psychologically, chronically incapable of learning to listen to how their voice sounds to other people. They just do not listen to what other people are saying about them and feel the need to reject criticism as a kind of persecution or attack. For that reason the criticism mounts up and in the end comes closer to the truth so that people become increasingly hostile to Opus Dei and it becomes less capable of listening and entering into real dialogue with other people of the Church.

It took five years after he left the movement for Dr Turner to adapt to Christian life and worship, following what he now sees was a nervous breakdown. However, like many other ex-members, he is not bitter but rather saddened that perhaps Opus Dei has lost its way.

Dr. Turner:

Opus Dei is an organisation which demands absolute loyalty. It produces in a person a very great state of intellectual and emotional dependence on the movement. To maintain its degree of organisation it has to get very deep into the minds, hearts and feelings of it members—otherwise they could not be held in. The walls have to be built within the person and the pressures build up behind those walls. I think sometimes, as in my case, the walls burst under the pressure

* * *

Opus Dei dislikes criticism, as Wicklow based freelance journalist Monica McEnroy discovered when she wrote an article in a leading Irish women's magazine asking questions about the movement's recruitment style.

Mrs McEnroy:

Some time after the publication of my article I was called in by the magazine editor. This woman was a superb editor—one of the best I have ever come across. She told me I was never again to mention Opus Dei in the magazine, and appeared a little shocked. The only way this could have happened is that she was leaned on from the top down. Somebody had decided that I was not to write about Opus Dei.

Following a letter to *The Irish Times* concerning Opus Dei's activities in Ireland published on 11 November 1982, Mrs McEnroy's contact with the organisation proved more personal.

Mrs McEnroy:

One morning, shortly after the publication of my letter in *The Irish Times* I had a ring on my front doorbell and was greeted by smiling Opus Dei members. They told me not to write to the newspaper again because the organisation would be very unhappy. I was amazed at this and took the view that it was a very amateur way of doing business. When they left I telephoned my local Canon. He was not amused to hear what was going on in the name of the Catholic Church just one hundred yards from his house.

* * *

Colm Larkin (not his real name) is a student of engineering at University College Dublin, and lives in Milltown, South Dublin. His family are a good example of what Opus Dei refer to as "family membership." His mother, father, two sisters and five brothers have been involved with the movement at various levels for many years.

Colm explains his feelings about Opus Dei:

For as long as I can remember there has been a very strong religious influence in our family. My mother and father are supernumerary members of Opus Dei. One of my brothers is a numerary and lives in the Nullamore University Residence. Both my sisters are nuns. Four of my brothers have been members of Opus Dei in the past but two have since left. I left the organisation in 1981.

My first experience with Opus Dei was as an eight-year-old schoolboy. I came into contact with the movement through the Nullamore Junior Club. It was a very active club. On Sundays we went on hikes, day trips or special outings while most other days were taken up with various sporting activities and regular religious tuition. My whole social life as a youngster revolved around the Nullamore Club and I was often asked to bring other friends along from time to time. As a teenager I moved on to the Intermediate Club. In this club there was more emphasis placed on study and religious practice. Friday nights were taken up by religious talks given by Opus Dei priests. The weekends were mostly given over to school study in the residence centres where one could be sure of peace and quiet. While studying for the Intermediate and Leaving Certificates at St Benildus College, Dundrum, my involvement with Opus Dei grew daily. Most evenings, after school, my Opus Dei friends and I would go to study in the Ely Residence Centre in Hume Street. At the age of fourteen I wrote to the Father asking to be accepted as a member. At Nullamore I was informed that fourteen and a half was the minimum age at which one could join the movement. As the years progressed I involved myself more and more with Opus Dei: study weekends in the country, a three week course on Irish at the Ballyglunin Conference Centre in Tuam and the biggest occasion of all—a trip to Rome and the prospect of meeting the President General of Opus Dei and the Pope. My parents paid for most of the cost of the trip but we were all given an opportunity to earn some money towards the journey. Some of those jobs included decorating the Newman College pre-University Centre in Merrion Square, painting the Rockbrook National Boys School in Rathfarnham and folding thousands of maps for the Four Courts Press Publishing Company. This latter job took months to complete but we were well-paid at the time. Eventually I had enough money to visit Rome.

It was a truly amazing experience. We travelled,

not as a group of Opus Dei students, but under the guise of a European Conference of University Students, all wearing badges to this effect. In Rome we met with hundreds of students from other countries and the atmosphere was of great expectation. Boys and girls were rigidly segregated. Finally we met the President General of Opus Dei, Monsignor Alvaro del Portillo and there was great excitement amongst the students. It was a great disappointment that we were unable to meet the Pope but he was unwell at the time, or so were informed. In Rome I was amazed at the grandeur and beauty of the Opus Dei World Headquarters. They were furnished with exquisite taste and obviously at great cost.

In the same year I took my Leaving Certificate examination but was unhappy with the results. I decided to repeat the exam and study at the Newman College Pre-University Centre. During that year I discovered other aspects of life I had never really experienced until then. I met some new friends, not Opus Dei people. I began socialising, going to parties, meeting girls and with all of this my personality opened up and I was more outward looking. Indeed, my whole personality changed dramatically. All I had ever really known or cared about from the age of eight years was Opus Dei, my Opus Dei friends and the strict religious upbringing. It was time for a long hard look at my life and where I was going. Eventually, I decided to leave the movement and wrote to the Father explaining my feelings. I left without any really bad feelings towards the Work and kept in contact with as many of my Opus Dei friends as possible.

I still believe in the basic aims and principles of the movement but am unhappy as to how some of these have been implemented over the years. For example, while I was studying at Nullamore a strict code of censorship was enforced. All books and magazines likely to be read by Opus Dei members were given a censorship rating from one to six. A rating of one indicated that the book could be read by anyone. A rating of two indicated that permission was necessary to read a particular book. Ratings from three to five would mean that these books could only be read by Opus Dei members of varying degrees of seniority. A rating of six indicated that no-one was allowed to read that particular book. In essence it was to be banned from the houses of Opus Dei. During my time at Nullamore, *Watership Down* was given a six rating as the book was deemed to promote abortion. The *Communist Manifesto* was given a six rating. However a specially re-written version by Opus Dei was available for students who were required to read the book for their university or college examinations. This type of attitude towards literature, I felt, impinged on personal freedom and bordered on anti-intellectualism. There were other aspects of Opus Dei which I similarly disliked.

In 1981 I was lucky enough to get a summer job. I was thrilled. It provided me with a new independence an my own spending money. On the day I received my first week's wages one of my fellow Opus Dei colleagues asked me to donate my wages to Opus Dei. He said the organisation had done a lot for me and that I should return some of that help. I declined his request politely.

* * *

The Byrnes (not their real name) are in their late sixties and they have two daughters. One is happily married and the other, Anne, has been an associate member of Opus Dei for over five years. Mrs Byrne takes up the story :

> Ann was an exceptional student at college. Her first job after leaving school was as a secretary with Dublin County Council. Following a brief period in insurance Anne took up employment with a major Dublin company and she was very well liked and appreciated by the company and its employees. Sport was one of Anne's main leisuretime interests and at work there were excellent facilities available. During the summer she would spend hours playing tennis, squash, swimming and mixing with her friends. She was a very sociable and outgoing person.

While working with the company Anne became friendly with one of the female supervisors, who was a member of Opus Dei. She and Ann developed a strong friendship and she was invited to meet Anne's parents on a number of occasions. However the subject of Opus Dei was never raised with them. It was many years before the Byrnes discovered that their daughter had joined the movement and how instrumental her friend was in getting her involved. They were further disturbed on discovering that Anne was passing a large percentage of her wages to Opus Dei. Over a short period of time her interest in sport diminished and she subsequently left the company to teach at the Dublin College of Catering, Cathal Brugha Street, while in the evenings giving Maths and English lessons to girls at the Opus Dei-run Dunedin Club in Synge Street. Today Anne gives most of her wages to Opus Dei and in return is provided with a basic allowance for her needs.

Mrs. Byrne is heartbroken:

> When Anne comes home from work each evening
> she is mentally and physically exhausted. We
> cannot confront her anymore about Opus Dei as we
> want desperately to remain a family. Before her
> move to Opus Dei our daughter was a bright,
> vivacious girl, very outgoing and interested in
> sports. Today we find her serious and withdrawn.

The Byrnes are fearful of their daughter's future. Both
want to make provision for her when they die but under
the present circumstances there are major difficulties.
Any monies given to her or covenants made could
eventually end up in the hands of Opus Dei. Mr. Byrne
wants to buy Anne a house of her own, or even a car for
travelling to work in, but this is just not possible under
the circumstances. He believes Anne would have
nothing to fall back on were they to die tomorrow.

Mr. Byrne:

> When we are dead and gone what can Anne fall
> back on? What happens if she decides to leave
> Opus Dei in years to come? We could leave her
> enough money to live comfortably for many years
> but know she would eventually give it all to Opus
> Dei. What a dreadful dilemma.

The Byrnes are ashamed to tell any of their friends or
neighbours that their daughter is a member of Opus Dei.
Those who enquire are just told that Anne is studying at
university.

* * *

One of the most common complaints from parents about

Opus Dei is the belief that pressure is sometimes placed on people to join the organisation Barry Crowley is a senior psychologist at St. Loman's Hospital, Mullingar and has written several articles on "cults" or religious sects and their effects upon people. To his surprise some parents whose children had joined Opus Dei contacted him to seek professional help. Some of the parents believed their children had been trapped.

Mr Crowley explains:

> When a parent is confronted with a very real personality change in their son or daughter it can be very distressing. I have seen parents who have cried, who got very upset, worrying over what they can do about such a situation. Often they tried to discuss it with the organisation involved but received no satisfactory explanations.

Barry Crowley has met girls and boys of seventeen and eighteen years who followed the discipline of self-mortification in Opus Dei using the *discipline* and the *cilis*.

Mr. Crowley explains:

> Parents can become very frightened when they see a young boy or girl wearing a *cilis* or using a whip on their body. My impression is that the infliction of this kind of physical violence on the body, under whatever guise, at such a young age is certainly unhealthy. If very young, impressionable people have been involved in this it can often create dependence and guilt feelings. This is one of my main concerns about Opus Dei. This type of self-inflicted pain leads to all kinds of problems later on— very negative attitudes towards the body and

the innoculation of guilt feelings about sex and other personal matters. It has been my experience that those who leave the movement often find great difficulty in making sexual adjustments.

Following Mr Crowley's participation in a BBC radio programme about Opus Dei in 1987, he was visited at St Loman's Hospital by a senior member of the organisation. "He came to correct my *misapprehension* about Opus Dei and politely suggested that it might not be in my best interests to say negative things about the movement in the future," claims Mr Crowley.

* * *

Peter Field (not his real name) is married and lives in Clontarf. His wife Susan joined Opus Dei in 1983 without his knowledge and it has caused problems within their relationship.

Mr. Field:

Susan was recruited into Opus Dei by a local Spanish lady and a group of her Opus Dei friends. She was initially invited along to the nearby Opus Dei club and developed friendships there. Most of her friends are married mothers and therefore supernumerary or associate members of the organisation. Never was I told she was joining the movement. Susan and her friends knew I would object and so they planned to conceal the fact behind my back. It is this which is perhaps the most hurtful aspect of all. Susan and her Opus Dei friends are often involved in raffles, sales of work, dinners and other events organised to raise money for the Rathmore Centre in Clontarf. On one occasion Susan came home from an Opus Dei meeting and explained to me how money had to be raised urgently for roof repairs to the Rathmore Centre. As she had previously told me that Opus Dei did not own the house but were renting it, I told her the landlord would be responsible for roof repairs. Never again was the subject mentioned. Since Susan's involvement with Opus Dei her behaviour has changed dramatically. For example, placing prayer leaflets all over the house and in our car; kissing religious pictures, crucifixes and scapulars; religious reading and meditation in the house; non-stop work; Mass each morning, even on holidays. When she and her friends come together in the house for prayer I am constantly treated as a bit of nuisance. As she grows in piety and prayer, I feel further and further apart from her and am disheartened with the role of the traditional Catholic Church. Her God and mine seem completely different. It is a source of great sadness to me.

* * *

Martin Reynolds is an architect in Dublin City.
Martin:

When I left secondary school and entered third level education I was approached by a good friend from my college days who knew I was interested in Spain and the Spanish culture. He invited me to attend evenings of song and culture in the Nullamore University Residence at Dartry, Dublin. I was attending Nullamore for nearly a year when I was asked to go into the study to meet with a priest whom I only vaguely knew. This man began to speak to me about my role in life and the importance of my work and how I could help God in my daily life. I was surprised by all of this—I thought I was attending social and cultural functions when I suddenly began to realise this was some kind of religious organisation. I was just twenty years old at the time. As soon as I became aware what was happening I disengaged myself from the centre but the attempts to get me to return persisted. The whole experience was a great shock to my system. To discover that I was being penetrated, my mind was being explored by a person who had me under observation at both school and college and who was hoping to inveigle me into Opus Dei under false pretences.

In a letter to *The Irish Times* on 13 May 1986, Martin Reynolds criticised Opus Dei as "secret, sinister, dangerous" and called for it to be "exposed and opposed." He said "if Opus Dei was open, its name would be on all its activities."

* * *

During the 1980s the worsening job situation in Dublin and throughout the country encouraged some students to work as language teachers for Opus Dei in exclusive Spanish schools. In the Summer of 1981 six UCD female students found teaching jobs through the Opus Dei University Centre in Clonskeagh. Siobhan, a student of Spanish, ended up at Mont Clar School, fifty miles south of Barcelona. She was not asked whether she could speak Spanish and was not provided with details about the religious group. She found the school system strange. The idea based upon a notion of "convivencia" meaning living together. What it amounted to was a grind in Roman Catholic theology, retreats and church services, meetings and discussions on sin. The other pupils were daughters of wealthy families and employers who were lay members of Opus Dei.

The girls lived in a rented boarding school under a strict discipline. Siobhan was not allowed to wear a bikini. Regular private sessions were held between the Opus Dei spiritual director and the pupils, but the teachers were excluded. The sessions concentrated on the evils of sin, but the pupils were forbidden to discuss them in any detail with non-Opus Dei staff. After a month Siobhan was happy to get away from the institution which she says "made normality seem obscene."

Her friend Susan ended up in another Opus Dei school near Vigo, in Northern Spain where there were thirty pupils under a directress and two assistants. She discovered that Opus Dei had a reputation in Spain for providing a "good education" and many wealthy religious families were eager to sent their daughters to the Opus Dei summer schools. While she had been told in Dublin that she was not obliged to attend the religious ceremonies in Spain, she felt alienated is she stayed away and eventually joined in the Rosary, prayer and meditation sessions out of "boredom."

During her stay a Spanish boy whom she had met the previous summer came to visit her but the Directress prevented Susan from leaving the school. In Dublin she had been told she would have free time, but in the school free time meant staying with the pupils and speaking English. When she visited a girl friend in Vigo for two hours on a Saturday afternoon she was told not to leave the school grounds again as the pupils would be jealous.

When Susan told the Directress that she was Irish and not a member of Opus Dei, and employed as a teacher, she was informed that she had no rights above those of the other pupils. Later her conversations in class were reported back to her by the principal. She was criticised for not speaking enough English while the Opus Dei staff who spoke good English always addressed the pupils in Spanish.

The only public phone in the school was permanently locked and it was only after repeated requests that Susan was allowed to telephone her parents. Even then, one of the Opus Dei members listened closely to her conversation. The following day she told the principal that she wanted to leave; it was agreed that she could go at the end of the week, but she was asked not to mention her departure to any of the pupils. She did however tell two girls with whom she was friendly, with the result that the following day the Directress stormed into her room and told her to leave immediately. The pupils were taken away on an excursion and Susan's wages were left on a table. She spent the night in Vigo where her money and passport were robbed and she had to rely on her parents and friends to return home.

Describing the Opus Dei set-up, Susan says : "It's not just a religious atmosphere but more a very intensive retreat. They take young girls who are malleable or even timid and they guide and direct them. The attitude is very anti-men."

Chapter 5

The Irish Experience

Irish people are no strangers to the many new religious sects which have visited our shores, set up house and remained ever since. Their purpose is to recruit new members, mainly those who are disaffected from the main-line Christian denominations and those who see the Roman Catholic Church as being unable to provide them with the spiritual experience they are seeking. Most religious cults take advantage of this and go to great lengths to align their public image with the main-line churches, especially the Catholic Church, looking first for an acceptance among Catholics, recruiting members in the subtlest of ways.

In 1982/3 an alarming number of cases involving religious cults came to light in the West of Ireland. As a direct result the Western Bishops came together for urgent discussions on how to tackle the impending danger in their dioceses. This led to the publication of the Western Bishops' Lenten Pastoral of 1983 which warned of the danger signs amongst cults:

1. If they give a picture of God that is very different from the loving, forgiving person who created us.

2. If they demand abject veneration for a human leader or suggest that he may be divine.

3. If they use the Bible to reject the church.

4. If they make salvation the privilege of the very few—
   themselves—and see all others as damned and lost.

5. If as a result of contact with a group, hitherto open
   and honest young people become deceitful, secretive
   and evasive, especially with their own families.

The publication of this pastoral letter provoked a
greater awareness of the dangers involved with some
religious cults. Whether Opus Dei should be included in
any list of cult groups is a question hotly debated by
members of the organisation. However, following the
publication of the pastoral, the Opus Dei-run residence
centres in Galway, Gort Ard and Ros Geal, were taken off
University College Galway's list of approved
accommodation.

One of the bishops who was a signatory to the pastoral
letter has since privately expressed reservations in
connection with Opus Dei's activities in his own diocese.
The real test for any religious group is the free will of its
members. No-one should be forced into joining,
remaining, fund-raising, begging, or hindered or
ostracised for leaving the movement. A solemn long-
term commitment to any religious organisation that may
determine the course of one's life is a major decision.
There should be an adequate period of reflection on both
the financial and personal commitments involved. If a
person decides to join, contacts with the outside world
must be maintained, especially with family and friends.
During recruitment, the name and principles of the
organisation should always be made immediately clear.
Secrecy and silence serve no good purpose and will

normally undermine public confidence in any such group. The right to contact family and friends in person, by letter or telephone must be observed. Telephone calls and letters should immediately be passed on without censorship or selection. Organisations must inform the competent authorities on request of the address or whereabouts of individual members and they should ensure that those people dependent on them and working on their behalf receive the social benefits provided by the state. Regulations are necessary to guarantee effective protection from any physical and/or mental coercion. A vocation should be a free response to God to a life of service, whoever or whatever you perceive him to be. On these criteria we are well placed to judge individual groups or members of such groups who may come our way.

What often leads Irish people to join cult movements and religious sects is a level of ignorance about what precisely Church teaching is. However, it is also unhelpful that words like cult and sect are used to denigrate, often without cause, perfectly legitimate religious beliefs and practices. Perhaps this is because Irish Catholics live in a homogenous religious environment and feel threatened by the unknown. Those with an inadequate grasp of their own Church heritage and teaching are vulnerable to subtle attack. Perhaps a greater degree of knowledge and appreciation of the Catholic faith is needed and the Church has to meet this challenge to survive effectively. Catholics are looking to the Church for interpretation, authentic teaching and practical application of God's word in scripture to their daily lives. Opus Dei claim they are providing this.

The organisation first set up in Ireland in 1947. A small group of Spaniards, headed by a young Spanish engineer,

Ramon Madurga, found a flat off St. Stephen's Green, Dublin and began a concerted drive to recruit members into the movement from the nearby University College Dublin in Earlsfort Terrace, the College of Surgeons and other prominent educational institutions around Dublin. Ramon Madurga was a postgraduate student in UCD and worked for a time with the Electricity Supply Board.

Opus Dei established itself by contacting young people and explaining the ideals and nature of the organisation. The group quickly made contact with conservative, right-wing Catholics in the Dublin business and financial community. *The Work* proved very attractive, especially to young people who were impressed by the movement's idealism and what appeared to be a new and relevant message regarding the role of Christians in everyday work and society. Members of Opus Dei were devoted to fostering the application of Christian principles in daily living, in all walks of life—it was an attractive prospect. This was the post-war era, the conservative ethics of the 'forties and 'fifties were prevailing and a new start for society was urgently needed.

Opus Dei's first residence was a house at 27 Northbrook Road, Ranelagh, Dublin. Amongst the Irish Founder members was Richard Mulcahy, a nephew of the former Fine Gael Politician General Richard Mulcahy. It is reported that when General Richard Mulcahy heard of his nephew's intention to join Opus Dei he threatened to burn down the Opus Dei house, such was his distaste of the fast-growing organisation.

Fr. Mulcahy entered the priesthood through Opus Dei and was the subject of intense speculation in August 1987 when rumours were rife that he was about to succeed the late Archbishop of Dublin, Kevin Mc Namara. Another founder member was Cormac Burke, a Sligo barrister and now an Opus Dei priest working in the Vatican. It was Ramon Madurga who recruited Cormac Burke as the first Irish member of the movement. In 1987 Fr. Burke was appointed a judge of the Holy Roman Rota by Pope John Paul II. This tribunal hears cased submitted to the Holy See either directly or on appeal from diocesan courts. Fr Burke attended school in Summerhill, Sligo and later graduated from UCD. He was called to the bar in 1950 and lectured at St Patrick's College, Maynooth, at Trinity College, Dublin and later at the Catholic University of America. It was he who carried out the first English translation of *The Way*. The final founder member was Daniel Cummings, a medical student and now an Opus Dei priest working in Dublin.

While the membership list of Opus Dei is not available, from a variety of sources membership in Ireland can be estimated at over one thousand, excluding co-operators and other supporters. Twenty-five per cent of these are numerary members living in the various Opus Dei residence centres.

The Headquarters of Opus Dei in Ireland is at Harvieston, Cunningham Road, Dalkey, County Dublin. The women's headquarters is based at Riversdale, Queen's Park in Monkstown, also in Dublin. Next to Harvieston in importance is the men's residence at Knapton, Knapton Road, Dun Laoghaire, County Dublin. The first Irish Opus Dei residence centre was opened in 1954 at Nullamore, Dartry, South Dublin. The official opening was attended by the Taoiseach, Mr. John A. Costello and the Archbishop of Dublin, Dr. John Charles Mc Quaid. Today it houses students mostly from the country or abroad. The Opus Dei Information Centre in Ireland is situated at 9-11 Hume Street, off St. Stephen's Green and this building also serves as a hostel for male students—the Ely Residence. The recently established residence at Cleraun, Foster Avenue, Mount Merrion at the entrance to UCD, houses over twenty students drawn mainly from the University and Dublin City. In 1957 the organisation expanded into Galway and opened a hostel at Gort Ard, Salthill to cater for students attending UCG. All these hostels are for male students.

Opus Dei opened the Glenard Hostel in Clonskeagh for women in 1962. This serves UCD, as do the Riversdale Study Centre in Monkstown and the Carrickburn Study Centre in Donnybrook. The Ros Geal Hostel in Galway was opened in 1972 for women attending UCG.

There are two conference centres in Ireland run by members of Opus Dei. These are Ballyglunin Park Conference Centre, Tuam, Co. Galway and the Lismullin Conference Centre, Tara, Navan, Co. Meath. The conference centres host seminars and study weekends designed to attract postgraduates, businessmen and priests to the organisation. Both conference centres and university residences have Opus Dei-run catering colleges attached and these are : Lisdara Catering Centre, Co. Meath; Ballabbert Training Centre, Tuam, and Crannton Catering and Educational Centre, Dartry, Dublin. The catering colleges are mostly engaged in training young girls who later work as domestic staff, cleaning and cooking, at the Opus Dei-run residences and conference centres.

The organisation is directly involved in education through two schools, the Rockbrook National Boys School in Rathfarnham and Rosemount Park School in Ballsbridge for young girls. For those preparing to attend university, or studying to repeat the Leaving Certificate, Opus Dei members are involved in running the Newman

College Pre-University Centre, 82 Merrion Square. The Director of Newman College, John McDermott, is a member of Opus Dei, as are a number of his staff. Newman College deals with students in the 15-18 year age group. It operates its own venture school in Wicklow and offers a wide range of commercial/secretarial courses under the auspices of "Institute of Secretarial and Administrative Studies," also based at the same address.

Opus Dei members are actively involved in running children's clubs in Dublin like the Anchor Youth Club in Artane, the Dunevin Club, Synge Street, for girls, the Harrow Club in Ranelagh for boys, the Glenbeagh Youth club in Clonskeagh for girls and the Nullamore Junior Club in Dartry for boys. Opus Dei is strongest in Dublin, Galway, Meath and Limerick.

Its members organise study weekends, seminars and retreats at the residence centres in order to attract students and other interested parties with a view to introducing them to the movement. The Cleraun University Residence Centre at the entrance to UCD is a popular venue for such seminars. In 1982 a two-day seminar, "Understanding Northern Ireland," was held with invited guest speakers, Austin Currie (SDLP), Raymond Ferguson (OUP), Senator James Dooge (FG), Seamus Brennan (FF) and Dr Cornelius O'Leary (Professor of Political Science at Queen's University). Later in the year there was a lecture on "Law and Morality" addressed by the President of the High Court, Mr. Justice Finlay and by William Binchy of the Law Reform Commission. Some of the speakers who attend such seminars may be unaware of the Opus Dei connection. For them, as invited guests, it is an opportunity to offer those in attendance valuable insights on a whole range of topics.

In 1987, the Anchor Club in Artane was the scene of one of Opus Dei's most ambitious projects ever. Growth had been cramped by the former facilities at 28 Upper Malahide Road, Dublin. They decided to move to bigger and better premises at the nearby Mornington Park estate and into the top floor of the old Saxa Salt factory which covers over four thousand square feet. The entire top floor of this enormous factory has been re-designed to accommodate an office, lounge, study centre, club room, oratory, store room, leaders' room, tutorial room, cloakroom and toilet facilities. It was a vast undertaking requiring a large capital outlay. Beside the new premises there is also a new workshop for young people built at a cost of over £150,000. A special Anchor Club members' draw was organised in October 1986 with twelve monthly prizes which included four Mazda cars, colour televisions and computers. Within a short period of time the club committee had sold the maximum number of tickets available, 1,500, at a cost of sixty pounds each. This raised close to £50,000 for the project. The former club premises at Malahide Road was sold for £20,000.

The Anchor Club was established to cater for boys in the North City area in the ten to eighteen age group. Most of these are schoolboys, apprentices and young workers. Activities are run by youth leaders—some of them graduates of the club—and by parents and senior members of Opus Dei. Three club members have since set up youth clubs in the Ballymun area. Amongst the activities at the Anchor Club are BMX riding, motor cycle trials, water sports, screen printing, computer classes, courses on study methods, music sessions and Christian doctrine classes run by Fr Oliver Powell, Opus Dei chaplain at the club. One of the main forces behind the amazing success and development at the club is leader

Jimmy Murray, an instructor in REHAB. His forte is in developing leadership qualities in the boys and organising most of the sports and training facilities. Most of the other clubs run by Opus Dei members organise similar classes but on a much smaller scale.

Funding for Opus Dei clubs comes from a variety of sources. For example, on 27 October, 1982 Mrs Maureen Haughey, wife of the Taoiseach, opened an art exhibition in aid of the Dunevin Educational Centre for girls in Synge Street, in the Bank of Ireland Exhibition Hall, Baggot Street, Dublin. Mrs Haughey said that since Dunevin was set up in 1968, the centre had developed into a splendid organisation. A report on the opening appeared in the following day's *Irish Independent*. The Bank of Ireland allows exhibitions in the foyer of the bank headquarters but usually the exhibits are just viewed. The Opus Dei pictures were priced for sale. The event was designed to gather funds for the Opus Dei Dunevin Centre.

On 7th and 8th March 1987 the directors at Cleraun University Residence ran a seminar on "Aspects of the Irish Media" with guest speakers: John Kerry Keane, Editor *Kilkenny People*; Richard Roche, Editor, *The Catholic Communications Institute of Ireland*; Eugene McGee, Editor, *The Longford Leader*; Ultan Macken, journalist/ broadcaster; and Fr Brendan Purcell, lecturer, Department of Logic and Psychology at UCD. During the seminar Mr Richard Roche told the gathering that a country's media, like its laws, should reflect the morality of its people. He said a survey of the divorce referendum coverage by the three Dublin morning newspapers had shown that all three gave "twice as much space to the pro-divorce lobby and attitudes in both news and features than they did to the anti-divorce people. The result of that referendum showed how ineffective this propaganda proved to be and how the three papers concerned got egg all over their red faces. This episode and a similar one at the time of the abortion referendum is reassuring." Mr Roche claimed that the media were ignoring the real issues in society and shying away from "close examination of the real forces operating beneath the surface." As an example of real forces in Irish society, this author has learned that Opus Dei members were involved in posting anti-divorce and pro-life amendment leaflets into public letterboxes throughout the country on the mornings of the pro-life and divorce referenda in Ireland.

Other activities have taken place at Cleraun such as : John Treacy giving advice on running in advance of the Dublin City Marathon; an orientation programme for freshers entitled "Who's who and what's on in college"; a seminar on human rights; medical ethics; music evenings and get-togethers with public personalities. Opus Dei make great use of the fact that such eminent public figures attend, launch or speak at their spiritual centres. For example, in October 1983, Mrs Maeve Hillery launched the plans for the Glenard University Centre for girls in Clonskeagh. This event received major publicity in the Dublin free distribution newspaper *Southside*. In February 1984, the Mayor of Galway, Cllr Michael Leahy praised the work of Opus Dei in Galway at a reception to mark the twenthy-fifth anniversary of the Gort Ard University Residence for men. In his speech the Mayor said that in a world where there are so many pressures, where materialism abounded, Gord Ard provided an "oasis in the desert." His remarks were publicised in *The Connacht Tribune*.

Opus Dei have many friends in the media and the

world of communications. Newspapers, radio and television have such an impact on people's lives and beliefs that it comes as no surprise to find the organisation have made major inroads in these areas at home and abroad, and continue to do so. There is nothing inherently wrong in giving publicity to Opus Dei and to the various centres and clubs its members are engaged in running. But avoidance of the real issues and activities of Opus Dei and articles written as a public relations exercise for the organisation can do a disservice to the truth.

In February 1984, Nullamore announced that it would be awarding two scholarships to students entering third-level education for the academic year 1984/5. The previous year's awards were won by students from St Peter's College in Wexford, Waterpark College in Waterford and Scoil Mhuire in Kanturk, Co. Cork. The awards, covering two-thirds of residence fees at Nullamore, were valued at over £1,000. The scholarships were awarded on the basis of an essay competition and an interview. The theme chosen for the 1984/5 awards was an essay entitled "Study as a Service to Society." One of the scholarship winners is now a member of Opus Dei.

In the February 1987 edition of *UCD News* an article appeared entitled "A Trip to Poland" by Joe Garcia, a third year arts student. At the end of this article the reader is invited to contact Joe Flanagan at the Cleraun Study Centre Dublin for further details. No mention is made of the fact that Cleraun is an Opus Dei Centre. No mention is made of the fact that Joe Flanagan is a member of Opus Dei. The report talks in very pleasant tones about the trip to Poland by some three hundred students living on a summer camp, working shoulder to shoulder with the local people, helping to build community centres of the outskirts of Katowice, a mining and industrial city of Southern Poland. The fact that Opus Dei does not always mention its involvement with various clubs and centres has long been a bone of contention with critics of the organisation. Recent times have seen the movement include on brochures and in articles the following line "Spiritual and doctrinal formation is entrusted to the Opus Dei prelature."

The Harrow Club at 39 Mount Pleasant Square, Dublin plays a major part in teaching youngsters in Dublin how to canoe. Founded in 1964, the club also lays quite a stress on educational activity and study through its involvement with Opus Dei. Courses of all kinds are provided at the Harrow and as a neighbour, the club has a special relationship with P. J. Carroll & Company who provide it with a perpetual trophy for a Slalom competition run each year on the Grand Canal. The Harrow is managed by a group of youth leaders and is affiliated to the Dublin Youth Service Council. In addition to educational trips in Ireland and abroad, camps and various sports activities are organised by the club leaders. The centre has three principal sources of finance: annual subscriptions from members, grants from the DYSC, and fund-raising activities organised mainly by parents and which to date have included art exhibitions, sales of work and sponsored canoeing events.

There are two other important areas from which Opus Dei look to recruit members—rural Ireland and those seeking training in the catering trade. An article on life at Glenard University Residence for girls appeared in the *Irish Farmers' Journal* on November 6, 1982 aimed at country students. It outlined the feelings of three students who paid compliments to the residence and its activities. The main point being driven home was that for girls coming to Dublin universities and colleges from the country, the Opus Dei University Residence was a home away from home. In the article, the Glenard Directress Loretto O'Connell was quoted as saying:

> We expect the student to study hard, and second year and third year students are willing to help them. But we encourage our students to develop interests in other areas and that is why extra-curricular activities are laid on.

In the catering trade, Opus Dei members are to be found in a large number of catering colleges in Dublin and Galway. Training in catering and domestic science is important for girls who join Opus Dei as many will go on to work as domestics in the movement's university residences, conference centres and training colleges. In June 1982 the president of the Irish Hotel and Catering Institute, Mr Colm Manweiler, was a guest speaker at the Lisdara Catering Centre open day in Galway. Lisdara is run by members of Opus Dei as a training centre for girls wishing to enter the catering profession. Another speaker was Mr Noel Duff, managing director of Buswell's Hotel, an employer of graduates from the Opus Dei Crannton Catering and Educational Centre in Dartry, Dublin. Buswell's Hotel was the subject of much publicity in 1983 when two lesbian nuns were refused accommodation by the hotel management prior to their appearance on the *Late Late Show*, on RTE Television.

Opus Dei is also a corporate body. In 1953 the organisation established University Hostels Limited, registered at 27 Northbrook Road, Dublin, to run university hostels in Ireland. Most of the Opus Dei centres are owned and managed by this company. A visit to the Companies' Office in Dublin reveals a web of relationships between those who turn up as business associates or co-sponsors of Opus Dei activities and institutions. In 1985 an application was made by UHL for re-registration as University Hostels Public Limited Company. The original Articles of Association of UHL state (article 89): "The President General for the time being of the Sacerdotal Society of the Holy Cross and Opus Dei, or any person nominated in writing by him, shall have power to remove any director from office and to appoint any other person to be a director." This article was recently deleted from the Memorandum of Association at a special directors' meeting. However, UHL is still strictly controlled by Opus Dei.

The subscriptions for shares in UHL were issued in May 1953 and in the inviting prospectus it was noted that the shares on offer were non-voting preference shares; dividends would be small and the company would always be run by Opus Dei. To this end, any purchase of shares in UHL was a financial contribution to Opus Dei. Of the eighty plus initial subscribers quite a few well-known figures at the time appear amongst them; John A. Costello, former Taoiseach and a member of the Columban Knights; Alexis Fitzgerald, senior partner in solicitors Mc Cann, Fitzgerald, Sutton, Dudley; Desmond J. O'Malley, father of the Progressive Democrats leader, Desmond O'Malley; Michael O'Reilly, founder and chairman of the New Ireland Assurance Company; Denis Burke, Clonmel meat processor and a Fine Gael Senator; J.J. Lynch, Chief Executive Mitchelstown Co-op; the Bishops of Elphin and Limerick Dr. Patrick O'Neill and Dr. Vincent Hanly. Three subscribers each invested £1,000 in 1953. These were the Irish Assurance Company (now Irish Life); Gerald Minch, Minch-Norton and Sligo barrister, Cormac Burke, one of the founder members of Opus Dei.

The founding directors of UHL included three Opus Dei numeraries—Cormac Burke, Richard Mulcahy and Michael Richards (Opus Dei London). The other four directors were the Earl of Wicklow, chairman of UHL for a number of years, with interests in land, insurance and publishing. He died in 1978. Another was Alexis Fitzgerald who represented Fine Gael in the Senate for many years and was appointed as special adviser to Garret FitzGerald's government in June 1981. On his appointment he resigned his directorship of UHL. In a 1987 *Magill* magazine report Alexis Fitzgerald said he is not a member of Opus Dei and has nothing to do with UHL or its hostels. Another founding director of UHL is Charles Brennan of Brennan Insurances. Mr. Brennan has been a director of the Educational Building Society, chairman of the Church and General Insurance Company and a director of the Insurance Corporation of Ireland. In 1983 he was chairman of UHL. Mr Brennan has stated that he is not an Opus Dei member. The other founding director was John Kenny. Mr Justice Kenny was a judge of the High Court from 1961-75 and a judge of the Supreme Court 1975-82. The Board of Directors of UHL has changed many times over the years. The last returns to the Companies' Office in Dublin listed the following as directors (year end March 1984): Charles J. Brennan, Insurance Broker and Chairman of UHL living in Dublin; Declan Bourke, architect, living in Dublin; Thomas C. O'Connor, university lecturer living in Galway; Arnold Torrents, engineer living in Dublin; Mark Hamilton, a manager living in the Nullamore University Residence, Dublin; Enda Bannon, university lecturer living in

Dublin; William J. Kiely, an engineer and director of Hostels Management Ltd, living in Dublin; Richard Magrath, accountant, living in Dublin and secretary of UHL, a director of Hostels Management Ltd. By December 1983 UHL had 145 shareholders from all over Ireland holding 25,000 shares between them in the company. UHL has raised substantial sums of money over the years to aid its development and expansion. Financing for the company from 1953 - 67 came from Irish Life; after that it came from the EBS. By 1984 UHL estimated the value of its fixed assets at £861,000. By this stage it owned properties such as the large Nullamore residence in the grounds at Milltown, South Dublin; the Ely residence just one hundred yards from St. Stephen's Green, Dublin and other valuable properties. Allowing for inflation, today the assets of UHL plc are valued at over £1.5 million.

In 1982 Hostels Management Limited was registered with the Companies' Office. The aims of this company are "to foster the religious and cultural development of men and women and teach the application of Christian principles." Very much like Opus Dei. Indeed the similarity does not end there. Of the eight directors and subscribers of HML two are directors of UHL, William Kiely and Richard Magrath. Hostels Management Ltd. is registered at Knapton House, Knapton Road, Dun Laoghaire—the Opus Dei residence centre. The other six directors of HML are :

Francis Curton, a manager living in Dalkey; Joe Flanagan, youth worker living in Cleraun, Foster Avenue, Mount Merrion; William Kiely living in Harvieston, Dalkey; Richard Magrath, an accountant living in Roebuck Road, Dublin; Con McNulty, an architect living in Dublin; Maurice O'Grady, a manager living in Monkstown, Dublin; Martin Ó Droma, a university lecturer, former director of Gort Ard (now at NIHE, Limerick); Patrick Ryan, an accountant living in Donnybrook.

By the early 1970s Opus Dei began to develop an involvement in secondary education in Ireland. The Educational Development Trust was founded to establish secondary schools for girls and boys around the country. The trust was to be funded by a new company—The Park Industrial and Provident Society which was set up in 1975. Three of the key figures in this venture were : Terence P. Horgan, Neil Dean and Gabriel Byrne. Terence Horgan is a director of Murray Consultants, one of the Ireland's biggest PR companies. Gabriel Byrne is a consulting engineer with business interests in Spain. Neil Dean holds a senior management position in an Irish bank as group internal auditor. Other members of the trust included Dublin lawyer Frank Fitzpatrick and Noel Duff, managing director of Buswell's Hotel. The Educational Trust has established two schools. In 1975 a boys' school was established at Rockbrook near Rathfarnham, called Rockbrook National Boys' School. In 1977 a girls' school was opened on Morehampton Road called Rosemount Park School. This has since moved to Ballsbridge, close to the American Embassy. There are some non-Opus Dei teachers in these schools. To get a child into either school today would involve an initial outlay of about £2,500 to enrol a pupil, plus yearly contributions and an interest free loan to the Park Industrial and Provident Society for the duration of the pupil's education. Today the Park Industrial and Provident Society has assets estimated at £1 million.

A major aspect of Opus Dei's media connection in Ireland is the organisation's extensive publishing interests. These are run by Michael Adams, a senior numerary member in Dublin. Opus Dei runs a chain of publishing houses under the name Scepter, the largest being in New York. In 1959 a company called Scepter Publishers Ltd. was founded in Ireland. Among the founding directors were Seamus Timoney, Professor of Mechanical Engineering at UCD and an Opus Dei member; Wilfrid Cantwell, a Dublin architect; Henry Cabanna, a Spanish priest of Opus Dei residing in Dublin at the time; Michael Adams was company secretary. The main aim of Scepter Ireland is to publish literature on Opus Dei for distribution in this country. However, Scepter Ireland has not traded since 1978.

The main publishing interests now appear to be operated by Four Courts Press, Kill Lane, Kill O' The Grange, Dun Laoghaire, Dublin. This company was formed in 1969 by Alexis Fitzgerald's firm of solicitors for Michael Adams, who owns Four Courts Press. The other founding directors were Patrick Holzapfel, an Opus Dei numerary and Donal Flynn, a chartered accountant from Sandycove. Mr. Flynn has stated that the is not a member of Opus Dei. Four Courts Press are the Irish publishers of Monsignor Escrivá's best known work *The Way*. They also published other Escrivá books, *Christ is Passing* and *Friends of God*. Four Courts also publish the Opus Dei *Position Papers*, pamphlets issued ten times each year dealing with various social and religious matters. The company has reproduced many works by Dr Jeremiah Newman, Bishop of Limerick who is a strong supporter of Opus Dei.

The Opus Dei influence in the Irish business community has been fostered greatly by its two conference centres at Ballyglunin and Lismullin. Those who attend the retreats at Ballyglunin normally come from Galway and surrounding counties. The larger centre at Lismullin caters mainly for the Dublin area. Amongst those who attend the conference centres are priests, prominent business men and politicians.

In the 1960s a fund-raising campaign was launched to finance the development of the large Lismullin Conference Centre. In the *Sunday Press* of April 30, 1967, Denys Turner, then director of the Opus Dei Ely Residence in Dublin, included the following as members of the fund raising committee: Cearbhall Ó Dálaigh, at the time Chief Justice and later President of Ireland; Sean Lemass, who in 1966 completed seven years as Taoiseach; Joe Malone, fund raiser for the Fianna Fáil party in 1981. Joe Malone has stated that he was never a member of Opus Dei and had never been involved in fund raising for the organisation.

Seamus Timoney, Professor of Mechanical Engineering at UCD, has been involved with Opus Dei for over twenty-five years. He ceased to be a director of UHL over four years ago. He is a numerary member of Opus Dei and resides at the Opus Dei headquarters in Harvieston. Timoney is well-known for his pioneering inventions in the field of high technology mechanical engineering, and his work on the development of a "ceramic" engine. It was he who developed the Timoney Armoured Personnel Carrier (APC) and a range of airport rescue vehicles. He has considerable business interests and contacts around the world.

The Timoney engineering group was born in a company called Industrial Engineering Designers Ltd. Formed in 1957, most of the founding directors of this company were Opus Dei members. Other Timoney companies include, Timoney Holdings, Timoney Research, Technology Investment Group and Techtonics

Research. Most of the Timoney companies are involved in research and development. Manufacturing facilities are located at Gibbstown, Navan, Co. Meath and in 1974 a company called Advanced Technology Ltd was established to run this facility. By 1975 the advantages of locating in a Gaeltacht area proved very attractive and the name was changed to Ad Tec Teoranta. The state agency Gaeltarra Eireann took a 49% equity stake in Ad Tec at a cost of £178,000 and made a number of grants available to the company. As part of the deal the then investments manager of Gaeltarra Eireann, Frank Flynn joined the board of Ad Tech but he later resigned. Frank Flynn was a member of Opus Dei at co-operator level. Timoney has strong links with the military establishment internationally. He had served as a consultant to the Pentagon in Washington and the Ministry of Defence in London. The workforce at his company Ad Tec is quite small—not more than seventy. Many of those engaged in the research centre are engineers and scientists from other countries including Spain.

In 1986 the Timoney Group showed a turnover of £3.3 million. As head of engineering at UCD, Professor Timoney can recruit the brightest people in the engineering faculty. In 1987 he employed the first, third and fifth best in the university.

As head of the faculty, his function would also involve recommending graduates to Irish and international companies.

Undoubtedly the highlight of each year for Opus Dei members is the annual Mass for the repose of the soul of the founder, Monsignor Escrivá. On June 25, 1987 the Dublin Memorial Mass was held in the Parish Church of the Good Shepherd, Churchtown, Dublin attended by over 500 Opus Dei supporters. Other Masses were held around Ireland, including one in Castlefin Parish Church, Co. Donegal and Galway Cathedral, all on the anniversary of the founder's death. The Bishop of Limerick, Dr Jeremiah Newman, was the chief celebrant at the anniversary Mass on 27 June 1987 in the new parish church of St. Paul, Dooradoyle, Cork Road, Co. Limerick. Concelebrating with Dr Newman was the former head of Opus Dei in Ireland, Rev Dr Francis Planell and Opus Dei priest for Limerick, Rev Dr James Gavigan.

Fr Gavigan is chaplain to the study centre which was established in Castletroy in 1985 by members of Opus Dei. The centre offers a range of activities to students attending the NIHE Limerick and Thomond College. The centre does not confine itself to the student body. It offers retreats, recollections and courses in Catholic doctrine and has recently held courses on the Pope's encyclical "Mary Mother of the Redeemer." Fr Gavigan is also chaplain to a similar centre recently set up by the women's section of Opus Dei at 5 Melvin Grove, Cahirdavin, Co. Limerick.

Introducing the 1987 Memorial Anniversary Mass in Limerick, Dr Newman told those present :

> We are gathered here to celebrate a Requiem Mass for the repose of the soul of Monsignor Escrivá. This is the first occasion of a public Mass being celebrated in this diocese under the auspices of Opus Dei. I welcome them to the diocese.

Speaking about Opus Dei, he said: "They have their critics, but these critics are false. They (Opus Dei) are strong. They stand for the truth—the faith—which is needed today." Those present at the special Mass included the Mayor of Limerick, Alderman Jack Bourke,

Mr. Tom O'Donnell M.E.P. and Alderman Frank Prendergast.

Opus Dei has met with mixed reaction from the Irish clergy since its arrival in this country. The late Archbishop of Galway, Dr Michael Browne, gave it his enthusiastic support and so the organisation developed relatively unhindered in the West. The late Bishop of Cork, Dr Cornelius Lucey, proved stiffer opposition in that county and throughout his long reign Opus Dei never succeeded in establishing a strong foothold there. Today Opus Dei is concentrating efforts both in Cork and Limerick. A small centre of work has been established in Limerick organised by Martin Ó Droma, a lecturer at the NIHE Limerick. Retreats are being held by the movement in the old Gougane Barra Hotel in Cork on a regular basis. Bishop John Charles McQuaid resisted Opus Dei's entry into Dublin at first but was later persuaded by Fr Alvaro del Portillo, the President General, to allow it to be established there. During the 1950s Opus Dei enjoyed the support of Dr Patrick O'Neill, Bishop of Limerick and Dr Vincent Hanly, Bishop of Elphin. Amongst the many priests who have lectured at the Opus Dei Lismullin Conference Centre are Bishop Donal Herlihy, Bishop Brendan Comiskey and Monsignor Michael Olden, former president of Maynooth College.

On 22 October, 1986 the late Oliver J. Flanagan T.D. asked the then Taoiseach, Dr Garret FitzGerald, if he had seen reports in the press to the effect that on his direction no member of the Government could be a member of Opus Dei or the Knights of St Columbanus. In his reply Dr FitzGerald told the Dáil that prior to his discussions with Ministers before their appointment to his cabinet he informed them that in his view membership of

Government would be incompatible with membership of any organisation, participation in which is by policy not a matter of public knowledge. He further stated that he had made no specific reference to Opus Dei or the Knights. In his view the public were entitled to know if a member of a government is a member of an organisation which by policy keep their membership secret. The discussion went on :

> **Mr O.J. Flanagan:** May I take it from the Taoiseach's reply that he was not by any means referring to the two organisations mentioned in the question. If that is so, I fully accept his reply.

> **The Taoiseach :** I do not know. I am not a member of either organisation and I never have been. I do not know what their rules are. My concern, quite simply, is to ensure that the business of Government is carried on in a manner that would command the confidence of the public. For that purpose, it is important that no member of the Government should be a member of an organisation, membership of which is by policy kept a secret or not allowed to be public knowledge. That would again be against the public interest. After that it is a matter for people to decide whether in relation to any organisation it falls into that category.

A new head of Opus Dei in Ireland, 38-year-old Dubliner, Fr Dónal Ó Cuillenáin was appointed in August 1987. Fr Ó Cuillenáin succeeded Fr Francis Planell as Regional Vicar, an appointment confirmed by the prelate of Opus Dei, Monsignor Alvaro del Portillo. Fr Ó Cuillenáin is a native Irish speaker and the second eldest of five children.

He attended the Christian Brothers Secondary School at Coláiste Mhuire and after graduating joined the engineering section of Aer Lingus. Before studying for the priesthood, he was involved in running the Nullamore University residence in Dartry. Ordained in 1978 he was later awarded a doctorate in theology from the Opus Dei University of Navarre in Spain. Before his appointment as Regional Vicar, Fr Ó Cuilleáin was chaplain to the Ely University Centre in Hume Street, Dublin. Paul Harman, the official spokesman for Opus Dei in Ireland, was a university contemporary of the new Regional Vicar. They both studied engineering at UCD.

In the summer of 1988, Opus Dei began to expand their base in Hume Street, Dublin. The organisation bought a large house adjacent to the Ely Residence Centre, formerly occupied by the Board of Works, to enable them to build another study centre and double the numbers they can cater for. Autumn of 1988 also saw the launch of a new magazine called *The Suss* from Opus Dei's premises at 10 Hume Street. The magazine is aimed at the student market and the editors are listed as Declan Mathews and Mark Hamilton. The Autumn 1988 issue carried a number of interesting articles including "Why Ireland should not decriminalise Homosexual Acts," a report on the Society for the Protection of the Unborn Child's (SPUC) court action against the UCD Students' Union for publishing abortion information and a critical look at Russia and the communist system under Mr Gorbachev.

Residences in Dublin :
Opus Dei National Headquarters, Harvieston, Cunningham Road, Dalkey.
Knapton, Knapton Road, Dun Laoghaire (for mature

members, male).

Riversdale House, Queen's Park, Monkstown (Headquarters for the women's section).

Nullamore University Residence, Dartry Road (for country and foreign students, male)

Opus Dei Information Centre, 9-11 Hume Street.

Ely Residence Centre, 9-11 Hume Street (for Dublin City and County, Male).

Glenard University Residence, Roebuck Road, Clonskeagh (UCD Students, female).

Carrickburn Study Centre, Seaview Terrace, Donnybrook (for females).

Rathmore, 9 Castle Avenue, Clontarf (for women).

Residences in Galway:

Gort Ard University Residence, Salthill (Male students attending UCG and Galway area).

Ros Geal University Residence, University Road, (Female students attending UCG).

Study Centres in Limerick:

Castletroy Study Centre, Golf Links Road (students attending NIHE Limerick / Thomond College).

Cahardavin Study Centre, 5 Melvin Grove, (for women).

Clubs in Dublin:

Anchor Club, Upper Malahide Road, Artane (for boys).

Dunevin Club, 38 Synge Street (for females).

Harrow Club, 39 Mount Pleasant Square, Ranelagh (for boys).

Nullamore Junior Club, Nullamore, Dartry Road, (for boys).

Glenbeagh, Clonskeagh (for girls).

The Helm Club, Galway, (for boys).

Most Opus Dei Residence centres have junior, intermediate and senior clubs attached for male and female members.

Opus Dei Members Working in Dublin Schools:
Rockbrook National Boys School, Rathfarnham.
Rosemount Park School, Ballsbridge (for girls).
Newman College, Pre-University Centre, 82 Merrion Square.
Institute of Secretarial and Administrative Studies
 82 Merrion Square.

Conference Centres :
Dublin: Crannton Catering & Educational Centre, Richmond Avenue South, Dartry (girls).
           Glenard Catering & Educational Centre, Roebuck Road, Dartry (girls).
Meath: Lisdara Catering Centre, Navan (attached to Lismullin Conference Centre).
Galway: Ballabert Training Centre, Tuam (attached to Ballyglunin Conference Centre).

Known Opus Dei Priests in Ireland:
Head of Opus Dei in Ireland:
> Rev Fr Dónal Ó Cuilleanáin, Harvieston, Cunningham Road, Dalkey, Co. Dublin.

Clergy Dublin Diocese:
> Very Rev Francis Planell, DCL,; Rev Daniel Cummings; Rev Brian McCarthy; Rev Dónal Ó Cuilleanáin; all residing at Harvieston.

> Rev Thomas Mc Govern; Rev Richard Mulcahy;
> Rev Paul O Callaghan, Knapton, Knapton Road, Dun

Laoghaire.

Rev Thomas Down; Rev Patrick Gorevan; Rev Martin Heneghan residing at 90 Foster Avenue, Mount Merrion Cleraun Residence Centre.
Rev Martin Hannon; Rev Eamon Sweeney residing at Nullamore University Residence, 26 Dartry Road.

Rev Charles Connolly; Rev Oliver Power residing at 9 Hume Street.

Clergy, Limerick Diocese:
Rev James Gavigan, Castletroy Study Centre, Golf Links Road, and Cahairdavin Study Centre, 5 Melvin Grove.

Clergy Galway Diocese:
Rev John Dudley Cleary; Rev Walter Macken residing at Gort Ard University Residence, Salthill.

The organisational structure of Opus Dei consists of a General Council—one for men and another for women, both independent and based in Rome. They are answerable to the President General. A corresponding organisation, a regional government, exists in each country, presided over by the Regional Vicar or Director. Decisions are taken by the General Council in Rome, made up at present of representatives from fourteen countries. The Central Council in the women's section is made up of women from twelve countries. The council sets down basic guidelines for the apostolates of the work around the world, leaving it up to directors in each country to put them into effect.

Chapter 6

Business and Battles—Controversies at Home and Abroad

While Opus Dei has enjoyed a slow but steady growth in Ireland, it has also encountered a stream of damaging allegations over the years. Opus Dei's Irish spokesman, Paul Harman, refutes all allegations that the movement is against anybody or indeed elitist. He believes a concentrated campaign has been waged against Opus Dei for a number of years by a small number of individuals which involves a "smear pack mailed to everyone and anyone." Three radio programmes on Radio Telefis Eireann in December 1986 highlighted enormous discontent and unhappiness among a large number of Irish listeners. Mr Harman refused to speak on any of the *Live Line* programmes, despite repeated requests from the programme's producers. In relation to this he explained:

> While I objected strongly to the erroneous and defamatory things some people said, I saw nothing to be gained by engaging in public polemics with them. Such a phone-in programme is, in my opinion, inherently unsuitable for dealing in sufficient depth with such topics. Even where I might be familiar with the particular cases, I would not have the same freedom to speak in public about such matters.

The initial programme arose because of the concern expressed to *Live Line* by a parish priest about an increasing number of parents seeking his help because of their children's involvement in Opus Dei. He expressed the parents' concern as being mainly with the secrecy associated with their children's involvement and with subsequent feelings of alienation perceived between the parents and the children. Independent research was then carried out on behalf of the series' producer, and this included a confidential enquiry made to a member of the Irish hierarchy. The Bishop expressed reservations about Opus Dei's recruitment activity in his own diocese. Following the RTE broadcasts, a flood of letters came in to the programme office, according to Marian Finucane, presenter of the series. Many of those who wrote in criticising Opus Dei emphasised that they wished to remain anonymous and that their names not be read out. After Fr Brian D'Arcy's participation on one of the programmes, he received a large number of personal callers to his house. Many of these were people concerned about the movement.

As a direct result of the *Live Line* programmes, a complaint was made to the Broadcasting Complaints Commission. The complainant, Mr Austin Keenan, Dundrum, Dublin said that a number of telephone callers to the *Live Line* programmes were allowed to make serious allegations against Opus Dei, the members of which were accused of alienating immature young people from their families, dominating them in a manner prejudicial to their interests and appropriating their property. Mr Keenan's opinion was that there was no direct evidence to support these charges against Opus Dei. In its findings in August 1987, the commission said that having regard to the repeated refusal of Opus Dei it considered that any imbalance that might have been apparent in the programme was not the fault of RTE .

In an interview with this author, Mr Paul Harman said that he had in fact arrived at the RTE Radio Studios to take part in the *Live Line* programme of 2 December, 1986. It had been arranged that his interview would be recorded for broadcast during that day's programme. However, while waiting in the foyer of the radio studio, Mr Harman met a friend of his who worked in RTE radio. He advised Harman not to proceed with the proposed interview as sections of the interview might be omitted and an edited version might not be in the best interests of Opus Dei. Mr Harman decided to leave without giving the interview.

Opus Dei has faced a number of battles over the years, due mainly to the revelations and accusations of ex-members—most notably Dr John Roche, who went to *The Times* in London with his private collection of secret documents. Dr Roche's article painted a bleak picture of Opus Dei's recruiting methods and internal practices. He has since described the movement as sinister and Orwellian. After more than a year of research, *The Times* published "A Profile of Opus Dei" on 12 January, 1981 calling for an investigation of the movement by the Church. This was followed by considerable media coverage, during which Cardinal Basil Hume was urged to carry out such an investigation by critics of Opus Dei. The Cardinal announced to the press that he would conduct an informal investigation in his own dioceses. Following that statement, the Cardinal received information about Opus Dei from all over the world and on 2 December, 1981 published his guidelines for Opus Dei which in effect requested the movement to discontinue any practices of secrecy, recruiting pressures, not to prevent members receiving outside spiritual direction, and also not to stop those from leaving who wished to do so.

Another prominent ex-member of Opus Dei is Czechoslovakian-born Father Vladimir Felzman, now working at Westminster Cathedral. In a letter to *The Universe* on Friday 15 October, 1982 he expressed a "sense of gratitude for what Opus Dei was and a deep, deep sadness at what it has become." He listed six reasons why he felt he could no longer continue within the organisation:

1. Young members discouraged from telling their families about their vocation until it has matured.
2. Censorship: Catholic press excluded from houses where younger members live. Bibles published after 1962 not used as "tendentious." Media stringently controlled. This all leads to a "cultural monasticism"; a *de facto* separation from and a suspicion of the world which the spirit of Opus Dei encourages everyone to love.
3. An intense suspicion of most post Vatican II theology leads the members to alienation from the world of everyday life. The past is idealised.
4. Meticulous suspicion of the opposite sex: source of temptation. The suppression of open-naturalness leads to imaginary problems which tend to become real.
5. Utter trust in Opus Dei's internal authority—theological, spiritual, moral, emotional, practical.
6. Total confidence in the founder's patrimony and thus a sense that Opus Dei is the reference point for liturgy, moral and dogmatic orthodoxy.

In his writings about Opus Dei Fr Felzman says:

> If, as I know from experience, Opus Dei is an organisation which, however noble the founder's intentions and high the original aspirations, has lately been motivated in practice by fear rather than love, surely the Papal approval implied in its new status might dilute that fear and perhaps allow it to become more 'Dei' (God's). As fear disolves, its leadership might open themselves more to reality and thus God, the Blessed Trinity.
>
> It might help Opus Dei relax, be happier, even joyful; respectful of the individual member of his or her needs in seeking their own salvation, life. Were this to happen—and it might if people pray (rather than respond to fear with fear)—the People of God would benefit, God has ways of drawing good, even from evil.
>
> As I know Opus Dei's history and the pain its members have suffered, I do not condemn the individual, but how can a priest in love with the open God of life encourage young people—or anyone for that matter—to a life whose characteristics are of martial law in a country under siege. What there is, is a sense of gratitude for what Opus Dei was and a deep, deep sadness at what it has become. Once again life proves that anything less than naked honesty has the taint of corruption somewhere in the shadows. Opus Dei does a great deal of good to those 'outside', but at what cost to truth, life, self ? If St John says, perfect love drives out fear, it seems that fear prevents—all too effectively—perfect love.

It was on August 15, 1981 that Fr Vladimir Felzmann drafted a letter to his "spiritual Director": "Now after 22 years in *The Work* and twelve years of priesthood, I have come to see that , though my priesthood is not in doubt, my membership of Opus Dei should end."

Another critic of Opus Dei, Maria Del Carmen Tapia, Santa Barbara, California made the following statement on June 15, 1982:

> In 1966 I was sent to Rome from Venezuela and placed under virtual house arrest in the Roman Headquarters of Opus Dei for eight months. It was never made clear to me what 'crime' I had committed but apparently as head of the women's section in Venezuela I had damaged the 'unity' of Opus Dei by winning considerable loyalty from the other members there, including some priests.
>
> I was constantly supervised, allowed no mail or telephone calls and I was regularly interrogated by priests and by my directress, and punished in many small ways. A sustained effort was made to secure an admission of guilt and a condition of remorse. My hair went white (I was forty-one), I began to cry at night, I grew thin and had spells of vomiting. I refused to admit to any guilt.
>
> While I was there, one of the younger numeraries from Venezuela, who was concerned about me, offered me a private box number in Rome, and offered to post and collect my mail. This was eventually discovered, and the Founder, furious, called both of us before him.
>
> My friend refused to tell him my box number and in front of me he instructed her directress to take her to a room, strip her naked and beat her until she talked. He told me I was in a state of mortal sin because I would not reveal the box number. I was then compelled to resign from Opus Dei. Shortly before I left I was forced into the confessional and

told by Fr Joaquin Alonso that despite a life of
penance it was unlikely that I would be saved. Some
years later I was exorcised by a priest of Opus Dei
who had been informed that I had undergone two
abortions and was 'possessed'.

On February 22, 1983, the national and international
business community in Spain was shaken when the
country's new Socialist government announced that it
was taking over Spain's largest business conglomerate—
the Rumasa group, which controlled nearly 400
companies in food, drink, hotels, insurance, banking and
employed over six hundred thousand people. The takeover was made to avoid the collapse of the group which,
according to the Ministry for Economy and Finance,
owed nearly £100 million in tax at the end of 1981.
Allegations of widespread financial irregularities were
made. The group President Senor Ruiz Mateos (Mateos
Rose) denied that his group was in dire straits and
announced that it was his belief that a campaign was
being organised against him. Senor Ruiz Mateos was a
devout supernumerary member of Opus Dei, and
Rumasa was heavily dominated by the organisation.
Following the death of General Franco, Opus Dei had
continued its influence in Spain's economic and financial
circles largely through Rumasa.

José Ruiz Mateos was once one of Spain's richest
men—until, he claims, he allowed himself to become "a
puppet of Opus Dei."

I heard that my companies were to be seized by the
government from the TV news broadcast one
evening at home. Since I had given millions to Opus
Dei and I was facing bankruptcy I asked the

organisation for help. They refused and told me to keep quiet and lie low, that they would fix it. Opus Dei arranged my escape to London where I had a steady stream of members, including clergy, visit me. The British Foreign Office secretly asked me to move on. They did not want to be involved in another Church-related scandal.

(Sunday Press, 25th May, 1986).

Mateos said Opus Dei functioned like a clandestine Masonic Lodge. He had been recruited into Opus Dei by two bank directors, one with the Banco Popular, and another with the Central Bank of Spain—both prominent members of Opus Dei. Mateos fled the fraud charges in March 1983, four months after the government nationalised his company. José Ruiz Mateos vanished just as Spanish police were preparing his arrest warrant. Mateos feared a plot to kill him by Opus Dei because he had evidence that some of his missing cash, about fifteen million pounds, was smuggled to the Vatican in a frantic under-the-carpet-move to plug holes in Church finance records exposed when Roberto Calvi's Milan bank crashed in 1982. Calvi fled to London and was found hanging under Blackfriars Bridge in 1982.

Calvi was a close associate of Archbishop Paul "you can't run the church on Hail Marys" Marcinkus, exiled in the Vatican after the Banco Ambrosiano affair (and replaced as Director of the Bank in March 1989). After his death, Calvi's wife told the Turin newspaper *La Stampa* that her husband was killed because of a deal he was trying to work out with the Vatican Bank and Opus Dei. Asked who she thought killed her husband, Mrs Clara Calvi said "I think the answer lies in the last operation Roberto was working on and for which he went to London—the assumption of the IOR (Vatican Bank) debts by Opus Dei."

The allegation is that Opus Dei would help out the Vatican Bank in clearing its debts in return for a stronger commitment by the Holy See against the scourge of communism, and more emphasis on traditional Catholic teaching. Calvi apparently went on a late night walk with ten pounds of rocks in his pockets, climbed down a complex network of bridge scaffolding and hanged himself. The scandal uncovered after Calvi's death involved the Vatican Bank—the Institute for Religious Works (IOR)—because its American Director, Archbishop Marcinkus, issued guarantees to Calvi in connection with the loans to Latin American affiliates.

In January 1989, a group of Italian judges concluded that Roberto Calvi did not commit suicide. The judgement stemmed from a civil suit brought by Calvi's widow, who is seeking to collect about £1.7 million on her husband's accident insurance policy with a Spanish company, Assicurazioni Genarali SpA. In their report, the Italian judges said that Calvi suffered from vertigo, making it improbable that he would have attempted to climb Blackfriars Bridge in order to commit suicide. They added that while Calvi probably arrived under the bridge on a boat during the night, it was unlikely that he was alone. One person could not have controlled a boat and hanged himself in strong currents. The circumstances of Calvi's death have also fuelled speculation that he was murdered because of an association with Italy's illegal P-2 secret Masonic lodge.

In September 1988, a Milan investigating magistrate recommended sending 41 people to trial in connection with the collapse of the Banco Ambrosiano. The magistrate alleged that the Vatican bank, which owned a part of the Banco Ambrosiano, bore a large responsibility for the $750 million in bad debts it left when it collapsed.

Under Pope John Paul II Opus Dei has flourished. One of his first acts after his election was to visit the tomb of the founder of Opus Dei and pray. When the Pope conferred the status of "personal prelature" upon the organisation, he gave Monsignor Alvaro del Portillo, the President General, jurisdiction over nearly 80,000 dedicated members worldwide.

Although the actual membership is Opus Dei is relatively small on a world-wide scale, its influence is indeed vast. The fact that Opus Dei shares many of the views and values of the present Pope has helped its progress and development inside the Vatican City.

Opus Dei, working hard towards the ultimate acclaim to the founder—his canonisation by the Pope—had sought the status of "personal prelature" since the early days of the organisation. But it denied this special recognition by previous Popes because 98% of the group are lay. The granting of the special status was a payoff for their considerable role in furthering the candidacy of Polish Cardinal Karol Wojtyla as Pope John Paul II.

The courting of Pope John Paul II by Opus Dei began when he was still Archbishop of Krakow in Poland. Initially he was invited to give speeches at various Opus Dei colleges and later at their headquarters in Rome. Many of these speeches were then collected in book form and printed by Opus Dei. On subsequent visits to Rome, Cardinal Wojtyla furthered his image by distributing copies of his book to members of the Vatican Secretariat of State. During his visit in August 1978, for the burial of Pope John Paul I, the Pope prayed at the tomb of the Opus Dei founder. In the Vatican, Opus Dei has replaced the Jesuits as the Pope's intellectual and diplomatic arm. The Jesuits had an army of 26,000 and a history of Papal association over a four hundred and forty-two year span but amazingly lost out to the Opus Dei organisation of whom no more than two per cent are actual priests.

In 1986, an Italian former numerary, Eva Sicilano, recounted her life within the movement to the national magazine, *Panorama*. Her depictions of alleged moral blackmail, intimidation, and forced alienation from her parents, led to a parliamentary enquiry.

It resulted in the Italian Government setting up a Commission to investigate Opus Dei and see whether it fitted into the catalogue of a secret society, prohibited under the Italian Constitution. A statement from Cardinal Agnostino Casaroli, the Vatican Secretary of State, to the Italian Commission made the following points in November 1986:

> Opus Dei is not a secret society. The duty of obedience concerns spiritual matters only. Its goals and existence are not secret. The list of members is usually secret but a ban on secrecy does not imply an obligation to publish. Opus Dei is part of the constitutional structure of the Church.

This was tantamount to a clean bill of health from the Vatican regarding Opus Dei.

Opus Dei's influence in the Vatican is a difficult jigsaw to piece together. Unlike other religious groups and organisations, members have no letters after their names. So basically, we have no way of knowing the full extent of Opus Dei's influence in the Vatican. However, recent reports show that Opus Dei are prominent within the Congregation of Bishops (which appoints bishops), the Cause of Saints (Opus Dei's main aim at present is to have the founder beatified) and in the area of

Communications. Opus Dei is particularly attractive to Pope John II because it shares his analysis of the present crisis within the Church. His concepts of obedience, orthodoxy and fundamentalism are very similar to Opus Dei's, unlike perhaps those of the more established orders, Jesuits, Dominicans and Franciscans who, to put it mildly, have been moved down the list of Papal interest. It has not always been so. Pope John XXIII was not a great supporter of Opus Dei. The organisation consequently accused him of being a rude old peasant and disliked his abstract intellectualism.

While Opus Dei has expanded in England, France, Italy, America, Australia and other countries, it has never succeeded in the Pope's native Poland. This is interesting in that the Polish Government would not allow the level of secrecy involved within in Opus Dei and thus the organisation can not exist. It has been claimed, however, that Opus Dei was involved in covert funding of the Polish Solidarity Union, up to 100 million dollars, via the Vatican (*Hot Money*, Thomas Naylor, Unwin Hayman, 1987) in return for open confrontation by the Vatican of the Communist Polish Government.

In 1983 the well known German Magazine, *Der Spiegel* published a series of articles written by a Cologne University student, Klaus Steigleder, who was studying theology in the city. Steigleder was a member of Opus Dei for six years but left in dismay. Following the *Der Spiegel* revelations he received a number of letters from irate Opus Dei members including the President General, Monsignor Alvaro del Portillo and the German Federation of Catholic Laity and Lay Priests, often referred to as the "holy mafia." Steigleder was attracted to Opus Dei as a fourteen year old but left at the age of twenty. His story caused a major uproar in Germany.

Since then, Opus Dei claim that a campaign has been waged in the city of Cologne and in the Ministry for Labour, Health and Social Affairs of North Rhineland-Westphalia with a view to preventing the work with youth carried out by the movement. The Westdeutscher Radio Station has been criticised as "unbalanced, prejudiced, tendentious, one sided" because of its stance against Opus Dei. There was public uproar when two Opus Dei priests were to be placed in charge of a parish in Cologne. Speaking on the controversy, Cardinal J. Hoffner, Archbishop of Cologne said:

> Would it be justifiable to place, as it were, a ban on the priests of Opus Dei, who are in communion with the Holy Father, and prevent them from working professionally for the Cologne Archdiocese? Certain elements of the media are very sensitive and quick to react to anything that smacks of an incident of "professional blacking" for political reasons. Yet they rejoice at the idea of Opus Dei priests being "professionally blacked."

The first major financial base for Opus Dei in Spain was through the Banco Popular. The appearance of Opus Dei members on the boards of some Spanish banks commences around 1947 but it was many years later before their influence became particularly noticeable. The Popular Bank of Spain was founded in 1926 and its founder and first president was Emilo Gonzales. By 1947 there was a major change of administration which shifted power into the hands of two Opus Dei supporters Fanyul Sedeno and Felix Millet Maristany. With Millet and Fanyul as bridge-heads, the penetration of Opus Dei members into posts on the board of administration of the Banco Popular began. In 1957, Navarro Rubio, an advisor of the bank, took up a position in Franco's new ministerial cabinet as Chancellor of the Exchequer, but continued to be a member of the board of administration until 1963. Between 1955 and 1961 the pace of development of the Popular Bank as opposed to the other big banks is astounding and within this short period of time it succeeded in moving into sixth position among the leading banks in the country.

One of the strangest incidents involving an Opus Dei member was that of Spanish national Gregario Ortego Pardo. On November 7th, 1965 a Venezuelan newspaper published the following report:

> Two bags with 225,000 dollars and a number of jewels valued at 40,000 dollars have been confiscated by the police, from a Spaniard who recently arrived in the country. The man detained is Gregorio Ortega Pardo, aged forty-five, and is presently in the hands of the authorities.

Pardo apparently brought the money and jewels to Venezuela to buy a building in Caracas. He had travelled from Lisbon on a British airline and booked into a luxurious suite in a major hotel in the city.

Following some intense police investigations, Ortega Pardo was linked by the Criminal Bureau of Investigations in Spain to the robbery of 300,000 pesetas from a jewellery shop in Madrid. Gradually people began to remember who Pardo was—Gregorio Ortega Pardo was a doctor of law, and a lecturer of civil law in the faculty at Madrid University. He was a member of Opus Dei. According to documents in his possession, he arrived in Lisbon in 1960 to found Opus Dei and established a number of residences there. Pardo was moving around and acquiring wealth in Portugal. He bought the agricultural bank of which he was President at the time of his flight to Venezuela. He developed a large chain of businesses in Portugal and was a big success— so much so that the Spanish Ambassador in Lisbon Ibanez Martin (Opus Dei supporter and Minister of Education in Spain 1939-51) decorated him with the great Cross of Civic Merit in 1963. Because of this Pardo's sudden disappearance caused an uproar in political and diplomatic circles. Was the holder of the great Cross of Merit, the successful businessman, the pious Opus Dei member, also a thief? At least Ortega Pardo was the same man who arrived in Venezuela on November 4th, 1965 and was relieved of money and jewels by the police. The Spanish Ambassador insisted that Pardo's presence in Caracas was to establish a new Opus Dei house in Venezuela. Stranger things were to happen. Pardo was expelled from Venezuela on November 12th to be handed over for questioning to the Spanish police. He took an Iberian Airways flight to Madrid. Asked by foreign journalists if Pardo had arrived home safely, an Iberian staff member said he could not confirm this as the passenger list had mysteriously disappeared.

Within hours of his arrival in Madrid the Spanish authorities announced that the police had nothing against Pardo and that he was not being sought. Following his arrival at Barahas Airport in Madrid, Pardo was immediately taken to a psychiatric clinic of Dr Lopex Ibor, a distinguished member of Opus Dei. At the beginning of December he was quietly deported to Argentina and given a new identify, but advised never to return to Spain. Pardo was a nasty embarrassment to Opus Dei.

In 1969 the Franco regime suffered another major

embarrassment in a financial scandal involving Opus Dei members and a textile company called Matesa. On the basis of fraudulent returns on export sales, Matesa had been receiving large credits from the Banco de Credito Industrial. The sum of money involved totalled over £75 million—much of which was invested privately abroad. Three ministers with responsibility for economic affairs, all Opus Dei members, were involved in the scandal and were dismissed because of the affair. However, by 1970, eight of the nineteen cabinet ministers in Spain—holding positions in Finance, Commerce, Industry, Development, Agriculture, Housing and Public Works plus the Vice-President and Minister of Foreign Affairs—all belonged to Opus Dei. (See David Gilmour, *The Transformation of Spain*)

Opus Dei's activities may not have received such a high profile in Ireland but the movement is actively involved through connections with individual pressure groups, campaigning for the conservative line on issues such as contraception, divorce, private health and pornography. They prefer to work behind the scenes quietly achieving their aims. The Opus Dei connection is rarely publicised.

When the controversial French movie *Hail Mary* (Godard's *Je Vous Salue, Marie*) was to have its first Irish screening by the Unviersity College Galway film society in January 1986 there was a furore. The film, a modern day retelling of the virgin birth by controversial film director Jean Luc Godard, was deemed blasphemous by the Vatican. In an unprecedented move the college authorities banned the screening due to the large protests outside the college campus.

The large number of protestors had been bussed from various parts of Ireland to picket the college on the night of the proposed private screening. Members of Opus Dei played a key role in the protest. Indeed a member of Opus Dei at the time, Sean Quigley, went on RTE Television to express his shock and horror at the film society's decision to show the film. He said that Catholics who trusted the Pope's judgement should rally round and actively protest against the showing. It was an excellent example of a small pressure group exerting its collective muscle on those who had exercised their free will to see a commercial film in private. In any case, unknown to the protestors, an alternative venue to screen the film was hastily arranged at a private house in Galway, an increased number of Irish film societies wished to book the film.

Back in Opus Dei's birthplace, a compromise between the Vatican and Spain's socialist Government in 1987 resulted in the Vatican agreeing not to choose clergy who are members of Opus Dei as bishops in Spanish dioceses. The "ban" was in return for an agreement by the Spanish Government to transfer its controversial ambassador to the Holy See, sixth-three year old diplomat Gonzalo Puente Ojea, to another posting. He was transferred under pressure from conservative sectors of the Spanish church because his agnosticism, Marxism and divorce worked against his remaining in Rome. The deal was also made to encourage Pope John Paul to make a third visit to Spain.

Chapter 7

A Divine Mandate?

According to David Yallop in his best selling book on the Vatican, *In God's Name*, no-one should doubt the total sincerity of Opus Dei membership, "They are equally devoted to the task of wider significance: the takeover of the Roman Catholic Church. That should be the cause of the greatest concern not only to Roman Catholics but to everybody."

Opus Dei believes there is much rottenness and corruption in the Church and that its members are the new chosen people. It believes it has received a divine mandate, through the founder Monsignor Escrivá, to recruit the whole Catholic Church into the organisation to save it from itself. Opus Dei is a vocation, an all-absorbing passion. As an organisation Opus Dei are kingmakers, encouraging obscure individuals to take up key positions of power and use their influence for the furtherance of the movement. It operates as a secret society, something strictly forbidden by the Church. The organisation denies allegations of secrecy but refuses to make its membership list or constitutions available to the public. Until Opus Dei opens its heart and answers honestly to: the widespread feelings of distrust, the accusations of elitism and secrecy; totalitarian control over members; discrimination against women; intense preoccupation with winning recruits; recruitment without the knowledge or consent of parents—then we can never know the full truth.

Most religious groups and cults have never generated such polarised points of view as are being expressed about Opus Dei. To understand Opus Dei it is important to understand Monsignor Escrivá. For Monsignor Escrivá, sanctity is the entire *raison d'etre* of the movement and that sanctity can only be found in terms of human freedom. However, any policy that deliberately prevents parents from taking part in the fundamental decisions of their children will undoubtedly result in controversy. It is the slow, unannounced transfer of fundamental loyalties from one's family to Opus Dei which has upset so many Irish parents. Yet many parents are intensely reluctant, even when their basic family trust has been violated, to cause a scandal or speak out against the Church or any of its institutions.

Opus Dei's recruitment policy appears to violate the spirit of Pope John Paul's *Familiaris Consortio* in which it is written:

> The right and duty of parents to give education is essential, since it is connected with the transmission of human life; it is original and primary with regard to the educational role of others, on account of the uniqueness of the loving relationship between parents and children; and it is irreplaceable and inalienable, and therefore incapable of being entirely delegated to others or usurped by others.

Anyone who has read Monsignor Escrivá's handbook *The Way*, cannot help but be impressed by the depth and profoundity of his Catholicism. But his book raises some fundamental difficulties.

Maxim 399: "If to save an earthly life, it is praiseworthy to use force to keep a man from committing suicide, are we not allowed to use the same coercion 'holy coercion' in order to save the lives of so many who are stupidly bent on killing their souls ?"

Maxim 941: "Obedience, the sure way. Blind obedience to your superior, the way of sanctity. Obedience, in your apostolate, the only way, for in a work of God, the spirit must be to obey or to leave."

Maxim 644: "Be silent. Don't forget that your ideal (vocation to Opus Dei) is like a newly-lit flame. A single breath might be enough to put it out in your heart."

Maxim 693: "Remain silent, and you will never regret it. Speak, and you often will."

Maxim 650: "There are many people, holy people, who don't understand your way. Don't strive to make them understand. It would be a waste of time and would give rise to indiscretions."

Is it official Opus Dei policy that "holy coercion" can be used in the pursuit of potential members or that "blind obedience" is required? Is it policy that speaking of one's vocation to Opus Dei is disallowed for the reason that the mere speaking of it will destroy it? How well prepared are the newly accepted members?

Of the "many people," holy people, who don't understand Opus Dei, how many are parents? Why would it be a "waste of time" to try to explain what is going on. And what kind of "indiscretion" is it that a "holy person" cannot understand?

Not to provide questions it to perpetuate a situation in which parents are somehow the natural adversaries of their own God-given children and that is unacceptable on every level of understanding.

Opus Dei will not be regarded kindly by the supporters of ecumenism. The movement's emphasis on traditional Roman Catholic teaching and Papal authority may have opened doors in the Vatican but it also tends to highlight more the differences between the Christian churches than those issues which should unite us. The right-wing conservative unbending stance of its members shows an unhealthy determination to hold on to the established order and a fear of social change. Fellow Roman Catholics are expected to accept, without question, the role and existence of Opus Dei due to its constitutional connection with Rome and the Papal approval given by Pope John Paul II. Any criticism of Opus Dei is seen by the organisation (and publicised by it) as an attack on the Church as a whole. This is a diversionary tactic to shield the movement from being questioned about its own failings and should be seen as such. Opus Dei's appointment as a personal prelature does not involve the Papal doctrine of infallibility. The Roman Catholic Church teaches that Papal pronouncements are infallible only when they are specifically defined as such. Infallibility is strictly a limited gift. The Pope is human and can make mistakes or fall into sin like anyone else. His scientific or historical opinions may be quite wrong and he can write books that are full of errors. Only in two limited spheres—faith and morals—is he infallible and in these only when he speaks officially as the supreme teacher and law giver of the Church, defining a doctrine that must be accepted by all its members. Opus Dei does not come within the scope of this.

Today, there is hardly a major city in the Western world which has not already seen the establishment of an Opus Dei centre. As well as being a major lay Catholic movement, Opus Dei is a multi-national financial corporation spanning the globe. What the final judgement of the Church and of history will be on Monsignor Escrivá and Opus Dei is hard to predict. There is no reason to suspect the movement will slow down its quest for formative minds, given the backing of the Catholic Church. But there is a grave danger, some time in the future, that Opus Dei may compromise the Pontificate.

BIBLIOGRAPHY

Main Literary Sources:

Conversations with Monsignor Escrivá de Balaguer, Shannon: Ecclesia Press, 1968.

Opus Dei Position Papers, Dublin: Four Courts Press, December 1984.

20 Questions to Monsignor Alvaro del Portillo, Dublin: Sceptre 1985.

Salvador Bernal, *A Profile of the Founder of Opus Dei*, Dublin: Four Courts Press, 1977.

Fr Andrew Byrne, *Sanctifying Ordinary Work*, New York: Sceptre 1975.

Desmond M. Clarke, *Church & State*, Cork: Cork University Press, 1984.

Rupert Cornwall, *God's Banker*, Oxford: Oxford Press, 1986.

Carol Coulter, *Are Religious Cults Dangerous?* Dublin and Cork: Mercier Press, 1984.

Josemaría Escrivá de Baluguer, *The Way*, Dublin: Four Courts Press, 1977.

David Gilmore, *The Transformation of Spain*, London: Quartet Books, 1986.

Peter Hebblethwaite, *In the Vatican*, London: Sedewick & Jackson, 1986.

Denis M. Hemling, *Footprints in the Snow*, New York and London: Scepter, 1986.

Dominique Le Tourneau, *What is Opus Dei?* Dublin and Cork: Mercier Press, 1988.

Fr Martin Tierney, *The Church and New Religious Groups*, Dublin: Veritas, 1985.

David Yallop, *In God's Name*, London: Corgi, 1984.

Other Publications
Richard Cottrell, M.E.P., *"New Religious Movements in the E.E.C."* European Commission.
Cardinal Luciani (Pope John Paul I) *"Seeing God Through Everyday Work"*, Opus Dei Newsletter, January, 1980.
Western Bishops Lenten Pastoral, 1983, *Renewing Our Faith in the Church*.

Periodicals
Gerry Flynn, *Young Life*, UCD Student Magazine June, 1982.
Paul Harman, "Opus Dei", *Reality Magazine*, June 1983.
Maurice Roche, "The Secrets of Opus Dei",
Magill , May 1983
Letters to the Editor, *New Oxford Review*, March 1984.
Covert Action Magazine, Winter 1983.(USA)
The Cult Observer, June 1984 (USA)
Union News (UCD Students Union Magazine, December 1985).
Irish Catholic Directory 1986/87.

Newspaper and Media Sources
"The Times Profile of Opus Dei" *The Times*, January 1981.
Also
The Sunday Press, Catholic Pictorial, The Irish Catholic, The Irish Press, Weekend Australian, Western Journal, The Irish Times, The Irish Independent, The Sunday World, National Outlook (Sydney), *The Catholic Times* (Montreal), *Evening*

Echo, The Cork Examiner, Der Spiegel,
RTE Live Line Tapes, Canadian Broadcasting Corporation
(TV) BBC Radio Ulster

Private Papers
Margaret Gould,"The Unacceptable Face of Opus Dei"
(England).
Dr John Roche, "Winning Recruits in Opus Dei."
"The Inner World of Opus Dei." 1981.

Other Sources
The Companies' Office, Dublin.

I would like to thank all those who helped in the research
for this book.